The United Sta

The United States Army War College educates and develops leaders for service at the strategic level while advancing knowledge in the global application of Landpower.

The purpose of the United States Army War College is to produce graduates who are skilled critical thinkers and complex problem solvers. Concurrently, it is our duty to the U.S. Army to also act as a "think factory" for commanders and civilian leaders at the strategic level worldwide and routinely engage in discourse and debate concerning the role of ground forces in achieving national security objectives.

The Strategic Studies Institute publishes national security and strategic research and analysis to influence policy debate and bridge the gap between military and academia.

The Center for Strategic Leadership contributes to the education of world class senior leaders, develops expert knowledge, and provides solutions to strategic Army issues affecting the national security community.

The Peacekeeping and Stability Operations Institute provides subject matter expertise, technical review, and writing expertise to agencies that develop stability operations concepts and doctrines.

The School of Strategic Landpower develops strategic leaders by providing a strong foundation of wisdom grounded in mastery of the profession of arms, and by serving as a crucible for educating future leaders in the analysis, evaluation, and refinement of professional expertise in war, strategy, operations, national security, resource management, and responsible command.

The U.S. Army Heritage and Education Center acquires, conserves, and exhibits historical materials for use to support the U.S. Army, educate an international audience, and honor Soldiers—past and present.

STRATEGIC
STUDIES
INSTITUTE

The Strategic Studies Institute (SSI) is part of the U.S. Army War College and is the strategic-level study agent for issues related to national security and military strategy with emphasis on geostrategic analysis.

The mission of SSI is to use independent analysis to conduct strategic studies that develop policy recommendations on:

- Strategy, planning, and policy for joint and combined employment of military forces;

- Regional strategic appraisals;

- The nature of land warfare;

- Matters affecting the Army's future;

- The concepts, philosophy, and theory of strategy; and,

- Other issues of importance to the leadership of the Army.

Studies produced by civilian and military analysts concern topics having strategic implications for the Army, the Department of Defense, and the larger national security community.

In addition to its studies, SSI publishes special reports on topics of special or immediate interest. These include edited proceedings of conferences and topically oriented roundtables, expanded trip reports, and quick-reaction responses to senior Army leaders.

The Institute provides a valuable analytical capability within the Army to address strategic and other issues in support of Army participation in national security policy formulation.

Strategic Studies Institute
and
U.S. Army War College Press

NEW DIRECTIONS IN JUST-WAR THEORY

J. Toby Reiner

July 2018

*****

Comments pertaining to this report are invited and should be forwarded to: Director, Strategic Studies Institute and U.S. Army War College Press, U.S. Army War College, 47 Ashburn Drive, Carlisle, PA 17013-5238.

*****

All Strategic Studies Institute (SSI) and U.S. Army War College (USAWC) Press publications may be downloaded free of charge from the SSI website. Hard copies of certain reports may also be obtained free of charge while supplies last by placing an order on the SSI website. Check the website for availability. SSI publications may be quoted or reprinted in part or in full with permission and appropriate credit given to the U.S. Army Strategic Studies Institute and U.S. Army War College Press, U.S. Army War College, Carlisle, PA. Contact SSI by visiting our website at the following address: *http://ssi.armywarcollege.edu/*.

*****

The Strategic Studies Institute and U.S. Army War College Press publishes a quarterly email newsletter to update the national security community on the research of our analysts, recent and forthcoming publications, and upcoming conferences sponsored by the Institute. Each newsletter also provides a strategic commentary by one of our research analysts. If you are interested in receiving this newsletter, please subscribe on the SSI website at the following address: *http://ssi.armywarcollege.edu/newsletter/*.

FOREWORD

Just-war theory has a long and distinguished history that stretches back to the Christian theologians of medieval Europe. Yet principles of just war must develop alongside social norms, standards of military practice and technology, and civilian-military relationships. Since World War II, and especially since American involvement in Vietnam, military ethics has developed into an academic cottage industry. As commonly taught to undergraduates and military practitioners, contemporary just-war theory seeks to ensure the political sovereignty and territorial integrity of nation-states. The theory insists that the only just wars are defensive ones and forbids wars of national aggrandizement. On this view, because of the right to collective self-determination, wars must not seek to remake the world order, as that would undermine state sovereignty.

In recent decades, however, cosmopolitan philosophers have challenged various aspects of the traditional edifice in an attempt to use just-war theory to enhance the protection of human rights around the world. Scholars have argued for greater scope for humanitarian intervention to protect individuals against their own government, for principles of justice after war to ensure that all states are legitimate, and most radically, for the responsibility of ordinary combatants to assess for themselves the justice of their military's cause. On this last argument, because combatants whose cause is just have done nothing to lose their immunity from harm, attacking them is unjust, and combatants whose cause is unjust cannot fight with discrimination.

This publication surveys these recent developments, and it finds that they provide a radical challenge to both the theory and practice of contemporary warfare. Of particular importance is its insistence on the need to strengthen international institutions, so as to provide combatants with an impartial perspective on their side's cause, and to strengthen military ethics education; this monograph also suggests that policies on dishonorable discharge be rethought. However, the monograph challenges certain aspects of the new approach, suggesting important connections between military ethics and democratic theory and practice.

DOUGLAS C. LOVELACE, JR.
Director
Strategic Studies Institute and
    U.S. Army War College Press

ABOUT THE AUTHOR

J. TOBY REINER is an associate professor of political science at Dickinson College, Carlisle, PA. In academic year 2015-2016, he was a visiting assistant professor at the Strategic Studies Institute, U.S. Army War College, Carlisle, PA.

SUMMARY

This monograph provides an overview and analysis of recent developments in military ethics that conceptualize just wars as a form of global law enforcement in defense of socially basic human rights and, in different ways, deny the sovereignty of independent states. Having first considered the arguments in favor of humanitarian intervention and for principles of jus post bellum (justice after war) that insist upon the rehabilitation of aggressive regimes, the analysis then focuses on a new revisionist approach to just-war theory, which it shows to be an extension of the other arguments. According to this approach, the traditional bipartite structure of just-war theory, which divides questions of military ethics into the justice of resort to war (jus ad bellum) and justified combat during war (jus in bello), must be abandoned. On this argument, the division wrongly absolves ordinary combatants of responsibility for judging the justice of their side's cause, as jus ad bellum is normally thought of as the responsibility only of civilian leaders. This increases the ease with which states may fight unjust wars and allows warriors prosecuting unjust wars to get away with murder. In the new view, soldiers become liable to attack in war only if they do something to forfeit their moral immunity to harm. This makes warriors prosecuting a just cause illegitimate military targets and emphasizes the gravity of taking a human life, no matter what the circumstances. As the discussion shows, this is an important challenge to both the theory and practice of contemporary warfare. It suggests the need both to strengthen international institutions, so as to provide for neutral judgments of the justice of resort to war, and to ensure that Armed Forces increase their focus upon jus ad bellum and the justice of particular causes within military ethics education. However, this monograph also queries the moral foundations of the new revisionism, and holds that we should reconceive just-war theory as a collective enterprise that is continuous with democratic theory, which suggests that expecting each combatant to make an individual decision about a war's justice may be in tension with civilian control over the Armed Forces.

NEW DIRECTIONS IN JUST-WAR THEORY

As conventionally taught, contemporary just-war theory seeks to ensure the political independence and territorial sovereignty of nation-states by insisting that the only just wars are those waged in defense of either one's own state or a third party that has been subjected to attack from without. Religious crusades and wars of national aggrandizement are, on this view, equally criminal.[1] The sole legitimate purpose of war is to secure a better peace than that which existed prior to war by ensuring the conditions of national independence.[2] While the purpose of just wars is to protect human rights, the fundamental importance of the right to collective self-determination means that wars must not attempt to remake the world order if that undermines the twin state rights of independence and sovereignty.[3]

However, in recent decades, a set of cosmopolitan alternatives to the traditional theory have emerged that have in common the conceptualization of just wars as those fought in protection of "socially basic" human rights, including security rights against one's government.[4] This monograph provides an overview and analysis of these developments, showing them to provide a radical challenge to the theory and practice of contemporary warfare by calling into question the legitimacy of the nation-state and suggesting the need to strengthen international institutions. The most focus and attention is directed toward a most recent development: the argument that soldiers may not rely upon the authority of the state to determine whether the cause for which a war is being fought is just, because soldiers who are prosecuting a just war have done nothing to lose their immunity to attack.

On this argument, advanced by scholars such as David Rodin and Jeff McMahan, individual combatants must be held responsible for participating in an unjust war.[5]

This position undercuts the distinction between the justice of resort to war (jus ad bellum) and the justice of conduct in war (jus in bello) that first featured in the just-war theories of Christian theologians from Augustine and Aquinas to Grotius and Vitoria and that has been the foundational distinction within military ethics for more than a millennium. For many decades, it remained foundational to the secular just-war theory of the 20th century academy. Most importantly, Michael Walzer argued in his seminal *Just and Unjust Wars* that there is a dualism between jus ad bellum and jus in bello because ordinary warriors are absolved of responsibility for judgments about the justice of their army's cause, but they are expected to refuse to participate in unjust actions during the prosecution of war.[6] As a result, there is, Walzer claims, a "moral equality" between soldiers: regardless of which side they are on, they may legitimately target each other, but they may not target non-combatants.[7] In large part because of Walzer's importance in contemporary just-war theory, for a long time, many scholars accepted this position unquestioningly.[8]

In rejecting this orthodoxy, scholars have appealed to a liability model of justified harm, in which soldiers fighting in defense of a just cause are immune from attack because they have done nothing to render themselves liable to harm.[9] This makes attacks on such combatants illegitimate. Furthermore, on this argument, the claim that only political leaders are responsible for such crimes does not hold up; obeying illegal orders may partially excuse combatants from responsibility, but it cannot justify their actions.[10] This argument poses a radical challenge to both the traditional theory of just war and the disciplinary practices of modern armies. By making the justice of action in war dependent on the justice of resort to war, it undercuts the distinction between jus ad bellum and jus in bello and makes the ethics of war all one piece, morally. It consequently denies the "moral equality" of soldiers, requiring combatants to assess the justice and legality of entire military campaigns, not just of an individual operation.[11] This means that it calls for soldiers to disobey the order to go to war if that order appears to be unjust, and suggests the need to develop accommodations for conscientious objection to particular wars.[12] Although some revisionists have shied away from holding soldiers legally accountable for actions undertaken in pursuit of an unjust war, the argument also points in the direction of strengthening global institutions such as the International Criminal Court so that they can prosecute crimes of aggressive war.[13]

The implication that international institutions need strengthening makes revisionist just-war theory continuous with other recent developments in military ethics, such as the insistence on a broadened scope for humanitarian intervention[14] and the focus on developing a set of principles for justice after war (jus post bellum) so that aggressor regimes are rehabilitated.[15] As will be shown, these three developments all argue for increased international scrutiny of domestic regimes and the development of a rights-supporting international order. Moreover, their arguments share a basis in the methods of analytic philosophy, and so tend to argue for just-war principles by analogy with the morality of everyday life. This monograph argues that this underlies both the importance of the new approach and the difficulties to which it gives rise. On the one hand, revisionist just-war theory is important because of its insistence that, regardless of the circumstances of war, taking a life remains one of the gravest moral decisions—perhaps the gravest of them all. Thus, one of the great benefits of revisionist just-war theory is that it pushes us to do more to try to hold armies accountable for taking lives by insisting that a defense of following superior orders does not justify the waging of aggressive war and only partially excuses it. On the other hand, the model of moral decision-making presupposed by the revisionist theorists is more atomized than is warranted. Worse, it may show insufficient respect for the norms underpinning contemporary democracy. Thus, in conclusion, while traditional approaches to the ethics of war may overstate the dualism between jus ad bellum and jus in bello, we may do better to try to incorporate moral deliberation about just cause within the training and practice of contemporary armies than expect combatants to weigh up the pros and cons of their nation's cause as isolated individuals. Put differently, while it is true that not all soldiers are equal, the argument here is that a broad swathe of combatants who represent militaries that provide recourse for selective conscientious objection and whose states ensure institutional consideration of the advisory verdicts of international courts are entitled to obey their government's decision to go to war without second-guessing institutional decisions individually.

This monograph has five parts. The first provides a brief account of traditional just-war theory, focusing on the arguments for separating the justice of resort to war from justified conduct in war. The second highlights the first two of the new cosmopolitan arguments, namely the need for humanitarian intervention to protect socially basic human rights and for principles of jus post bellum that would rehabilitate aggressor regimes. The third directs careful attention on revisionist just-war theory's rejection of the moral equality of soldiers and insistence that combatants must judge for themselves the justice of their army's resort to war. The fourth assesses the new approaches, arguing that democratic participation in decisions to go to war is preferable to expecting each combatant to make her or his own judgment. The final section notes the implications of this analysis for the theory and practice of war, including the importance of strengthening global institutions so that combatants have some notion of the justice of their country's cause as judged by a third party. Militaries should rethink their policies on dishonorable discharge to accommodate selective conscientious objection and that military ethics are a particular form of role morality. There is an urgent need to change the education in senior service schools so as both to integrate the ethics of war with strategic objectives and to provide greater focus on jus ad bellum. Furthermore, military ethics should incorporate consideration of its relationship to democratic theory.

TRADITIONAL JUST-WAR THEORY

The foundational distinction in most versions of just-war theory is the one that revisionism seeks to reject—that between jus ad bellum and jus in bello. For example, many theorists have argued that, for the resort to war to be justified, there must be a just cause, reasonable possibility of success, and public declaration of war by a competent authority, while the war must also be a last resort that is proportionate in its ends.[16] Regarding the means deployed in war, most ethicists have taken the crucial principles to be proportionality of means and discrimination[17] (usually taken to mean respecting non-combatant immunity).[18] A similar division was also present in the just-war theories of the Christian jurists of medieval and early-modern Europe.[19] Underlying the division of just-war theory into jus ad bellum and jus in bello is the claim that the moral principles appropriate to the decision to resort to war are of a different order to those governing action in war because of the difference in context. Jus ad bellum is the responsibility of political, and sometimes military, leaders; ordinary combatants are not responsible for jus ad bellum and must abide only by the principles of jus in bello. As a result, the same principles of jus in bello apply to all soldiers, regardless of the cause for which they are fighting. An allied soldier in World War II was on the same moral footing as a Nazi, if both obeyed the principles of jus in bello. As David Rodin puts it, two theses underlie this argument: first, a symmetry thesis that states that all combatants have the same jus in bello rights and obligations; second, an independence thesis, which suggests that those rights and obligations are independent of the justice of the war being fought.[20] Both theses lead to the conclusion that there is a "moral equality of soldiers."[21]

In recent just-war theory, the most important defenses of these claims are those provided by Michael Walzer. In *Just and Unjust Wars*, Walzer argues for a "dualism" between the two parts of just-war theory because part of the crime that is aggressive war consists of making warriors into "human instruments" trapped in a war not of their own making.[22] Soldiers are moral equals because of their shared victimhood at the hands of the state that corrals them into fighting to further causes of its own. War really would be hell, Walzer argues, if this coercion, and the risks to which it subjects soldiers, did not bring in its wake certain rights, in particular the right to kill enemy combatants without being accused of the crime of aggressive war, ameliorating soldiers' situation somewhat. Further-more, Walzer grounds the moral equality of soldiers in the facts that "they are led to fight by their loyalty to their own states and by their lawful obedience. They are most likely to believe that their wars are just."[23] That this belief is not based on "rational inquiry," but "a kind of unquestioning acceptance of official propa-ganda," does not make such soldiers criminals.[24] Even were soldiers to seek to question the state's claims, they would often be incapable of discerning the truth of the situation. Combatants have, so to speak, an invincible ignorance of the justice of their army's war. Walzer insists that the moral equality of soldiers applies to all Armed Forces, even those of Nazi Germany, if they abide by the principles of jus in bello.[25]

It is worth noting that Walzer considers only reject-ing an alternative to the moral equality of soldiers, which he names the "sliding scale" approach.[26] This is the view that an army fighting for a just cause has more right on its side than its opponents and may fight less discriminately than the opponents may. Walzer rejects the sliding scale because it would erode the war convention and make it easier for leaders to believe that they are forced to violate human rights.[27] The sliding-scale approach would introduce an element of asymmetry into just-war theory by suggesting that soldiers do not all have the same rights. It would also undercut what Rodin called the independence thesis, by basing that asymmetry on the justice of the cause that soldiers seek to uphold. However, Walzer only considers one form of asymmetry, which Rodin later called "permissive asymmetry." This is the view that just warriors have rights to violate jus in bello prin-ciples. Walzer does not consider "restrictive asymme-try," which would have denied to unjust warriors the right to kill at all and held that combatants fighting for a just cause may attack enemy soldiers but must respect jus in bello principles.[28] In essence, revisionist just-war theory is the view that, while Walzer was right to reject permissive asymmetry, he ought not to have rejected asymmetry per se but, instead, denied war rights to combatants whose cause is unjust.

Indeed, Walzer does not ultimately maintain an absolute form of the independence thesis. As soon as he rejects the sliding-scale approach, he goes on to acknowledge that there may be situations in which it is so important that the just side win the war that they must be granted leeway to violate principles of jus in bello. Walzer calls such situations "supreme emergencies"[29] and argues that they arise when there is a "threat to human values so radical that its imminence"[30] and its seriousness combine to warrant an army to do whatever it must do to avert the threat, including, if necessary, deliberately targeting civilians. Space precludes consideration of the merits of this argument here, which has also proven highly controversial.[31] However, it is worth bearing in mind that most theories of just war seek to find a way to ensure that the just side is more likely to win the war, at least in extreme circumstances, and that it is not only revisionists who are uncomfortable with the idea that war rights are independent of just cause.

THE MOVEMENT TOWARD COSMOPOLITAN JUST-WAR THEORY

Challenging the Paradigm: The Argument for Humanitarian Intervention

The new directions in just-war theory share a concern to reduce the incidence of justice in warfare by bolstering the denial of the right to use force to those who would not have a just cause on their side. As we shall see, this trend reaches its apotheosis in revisionist just-war theory, which extends that denial to ordinary warriors who obey the principles of jus in bello but whose military's cause is unjust. However, the first movements in this direction targeted not combatants, but the state, whose rights to territorial integrity and political sovereignty were denied by a wave of cosmopolitan critics of Walzer's *Just and Unjust Wars* in the late 1970s. These arguments laid the theoretical foundations for subsequent developments in military practice such as the notion that there is a responsibility to protect human rights wherever violations occur. These critics followed Walzer in insisting that individual human rights must be the foundation of principles of just war and that only defensive wars can be just. Where Walzer's early critics broke with him was on the claim that the only legitimate defensive wars were wars of national defense.[32] Rather, they held, if just-war theory is grounded in human rights, then those must include rights against one's own government, which means that humanitarian interventions can be justified on the grounds that they defend the rights of the persecuted, even though no national boundary has been breached.[33] Where Walzer, following John Mill, had accepted humanitarian intervention only in very limited circumstances, the critics were more concerned to avoid the danger of states violating the rights of their citizens.

In response, Walzer argued that, while it was true that states that committed human rights violations were illegitimate from the point of view of their own citizens, just-war theorists should, for the most part, presume a "fit" between government and citizen body. This means that humanitarian intervention should take place only to prevent massacre or slavery or as a form of counterintervention in civil wars.[34] According to this argument, just-war theory should not seek to remake the world order such that states are reconstituted as liberal democracies; rather, state rights to territorial integrity and political sovereignty exist because these are necessary for individuals to establish common lives in communities of their own.[35] It is this right to collective self-determination that undergirds what Walzer calls the "legalist paradigm," in which the rights of states are justified by virtue of a "domestic analogy" with individual rights.[36] In order to ensure the individual right to collective self-determination, states have equal rights, although they can lose those rights by acts of aggression, as can individuals. Similarly, absent acts of aggression, the rights of states must be respected, and thus just-war theory cannot be used to attempt to justify the forcible reconstruction of states by "authorities who stand outside the political arena."[37]

However, this response did not satisfy Walzer's critics, who held that his view seemed "to privilege the value of communal integrity and give insufficient weight to human rights."[38] They argued that just wars should not be conceived of as ones fought in defense of the political sovereignty and territorial integrity of independent states representing distinct communities, but rather as defenses of "socially basic human rights," including security rights against one's government.[39] The entitlement to prosecute wars in defense of basic rights stems from the fact that such rights have a "cosmopolitan nature," as they are "necessary for the enjoyment of any other rights at all"; because people cannot survive without them, basic rights are "universal."[40] Defense of basic rights is therefore incompatible with national sovereignty that critics hold to be "indifferent" to basic rights and based on a "myth" of national commonality.[41] On this view, just-war theory must dispense with the domestic analogy and proceed as though state rights are justified only when states uphold socially basic human rights. When they do not do so, states should be taken to be illegitimate and lose their rights to sovereignty. This means that the argument for humanitarian intervention forms part of a conception of just wars that, at least in embryonic form, partakes in the cosmopolitan project of seeking to remake the world order such that basic rights are respected everywhere. For this reason, although Walzer's early critics did not adopt the liability model that calls into question the dualism between jus ad bellum and jus in bello, we should understand them as taking the first important steps toward it in conceptualizing just wars as a form of global law enforcement.

Vignette 1: Humanitarian Intervention

National Sovereignty versus Individual Rights: Apartheid South Africa and the Sandinistas in Nicaragua

Many real-world cases of humanitarian intervention are ones for which both traditional just-war theorists and their cosmopolitan critics who, as noted in the main text, argue against a strong right to national sovereignty and come to similar policy conclusions. For example, there was a moral case for intervention in apartheid South Africa according to both types of just-war theory, albeit on different grounds. Cosmopolitans treated apartheid as an example of oppression that warranted intervention because the rights of black South Africans were being violated. For advocates of the traditional approach, on the other hand, to talk in terms of "oppression" was to miss the severity of the situation and the fact that black South Africans took their struggle to be one against something that amounted in effect to slavery and to be a struggle for national liberation.

However, there are situations in which the different approaches come to different conclusions about whether intervention is warranted. An important example here is the case of the Nicaraguan Sandinistas. Cosmopolitan theory probably suggests that there should have been a foreign intervention in Nicaragua at the time of the first Sandinista struggle against the Anastasio Somoza regime in 1978, whereas according to the traditional theory, such an intervention would not have been warranted. The reason for this is that intervention would have exempted the Sandinistas from having to engage in an internal bargaining about the character of the new regime that they would establish upon taking power. According to Walzer, humanitarian intervention in 1978 would have "violated the right of Nicaraguans as a group to shape their own political institutions," and doing so would have interfered with the collective right to self-determination of the Nicaraguan people.[42]

What this means is that in cases where humanitarian intervention may appear to be called for, it is important for intervening powers to consider which rights are at stake in a particular case. On the traditional just-war approach, humanitarian intervention does not only protect rights, it also endangers them, because it runs the risk of establishing a satellite power that is not in any meaningful sense a local regime. On the cosmopolitan approach of more recent just-war theory, this suggestion overstates the importance of the nation-state and so gives insufficient weight to individual human rights. What militaries must consider, then, is how important such things as national independence are to black South Africans and oppressed Nicaraguans compared to relief from violent rights-violations.[43]

The Addition of Jus Post Bellum

The next major development in cosmopolitan just-war thinking occurred around the turn of the millennium.[44] At that time, the geopolitical climate of the post-Cold War world, which led to a renewal of ethnic conflict across both Europe and sub-Saharan Africa, encouraged a new generation of theorists to argue that justice after war—jus post bellum—must be considered an independent part of just-war theory, and could no longer be subsumed into jus ad bellum and jus in bello. Both the increased need for humanitarian intervention and the use of military force in "chaotic arenas of insecurity" meant that independent principles of post-war settlements were major requirements of military ethics.[45] More recently, the wars of regime change—whether justified or not—need the guidance of a set of post-conflict principles that can avert the danger of descent into chaos. As a result, theorists of jus post bellum have continued the cosmopolitan project of treating just-war theory as a form of global law enforcement by arguing that just wars must aim at creating just societies, and that just-war theory must be linked to theorizing about justice in domestic society. Not to do so is to downplay the "ethical implications of the status quo."[46] Doing so misses the opportunity to help contribute to a more peaceful and just world.

To see why scholars conclude that the absence of principles tailored specifically to jus post bellum is a major omission, let us consider the traditional view. Walzer is again paradigmatic. In the late 1970s, he followed the traditional just-war paradigm in assuming that all that justice after war required was a "better peace" than the status quo prior to war, where better means "more secure than the *status quo ante bellum*, less vulnerable to territorial expansion, safer for ordinary men and women and for their domestic self-determinations [italics in original]."[47] Walzer is explicit that these words must be used relatively; it can be no part of just-war theory to try to ensure perfect safety, whatever that might mean, because "Just wars are limited wars."[48] The limits in this instance relate to the ends of war, and not just to its means. Walzer holds that the "theory of ends in war is shaped by the same rights that justify the fighting in the first place—most importantly, by the rights of nations, even of enemy nations, to continued national existence and, except in extreme circumstances, to the political prerogatives of nationality."[49] Justice after war requires a more secure status quo, such that the conditions that caused the war might be changed so that a new war does not follow quickly upon the cessation of the old. It cannot require the remaking of the world order and of the internal politics of nations such that we encourage the spread of liberal democracy. National self-determination, on this view, has its limits, but it should not be interpreted as requiring similar political forms all over the world. Extending this principle, Walzer argued that, in those exceptional cases of humanitarian intervention that he did accept, the intervention concluded with the cessation of rights-violations, and did not require democratization. Interveners should be guided by a rule of "in and quickly out."[50]

Walzer's view is, as usual, the received one,[51] but even when he wrote *Just and Unjust Wars*, the legal situation had departed from the traditional just-war view.[52] The experience of Nazism had led to the establishment of post-war military tribunals to deal with crimes against humanity and the like.[53] Walzer discusses the Nuremberg trials, but he treats the issue as a matter of allocating responsibility for crimes of war, introducing it in cohort with an account of responsibility for American involvement in Vietnam, rather than as a separate branch of just-war theory.[54] This may be because of his appeal to the legalist paradigm, which pictures states as perpetually in tension with each other and suggests that just-war theory should focus on restraint of states and not on transformation of the state system.[55] Cosmopolitan advocates of jus post bellum have rejected this claim, arguing that we need to rethink the belief that "the end of war is a better state of peace" and replace it with a view that sees just wars as part of a progressive transformation of the state system toward one of global respect for human rights.[56] In partial acceptance of this, Walzer has revised the rule that should guide humanitarian intervention to "in and finally out," once independent local authorities are securely in place,[57] arguing that jus post bellum reflects the need for war to aim at "social justice in its minimal sense: the creation of a safe and decent society."[58]

Advocates of jus post bellum, then, reject the legalist paradigm that guides traditional just-war theory in favor of a model of rehabilitation that seeks to ensure that aggressor regimes are reconstituted such that they become "progressive member[s] of the international community."[59] The legalist paradigm, in treating punishment for war crimes as a matter of allocating responsibility for war crimes, on this view does not pay sufficient attention to the need for conciliation and security after war.[60] At the least, it fails to recognize that long-term security requires societies that are more just. Brian Orend argues that the traditional model treats postwar justice as a matter of revenge, seeing postwar peace as involving an apology from the aggressor, war crimes tribunals for those responsible, demilitarization, the giving up of territorial gains, and possibly further losses.[61] Orend cites the Paris Peace Treaties that ended World War I and the treaty that ended the first Gulf war as examples of this model.[62] By contrast, Orend argues, a rehabilitative model of jus post bellum requires something more like the peace treaties that ended World War II. Rehabilitation does not mean the eschewal of apologies, demilitarization, and war crimes tribunals, but it does reject sanctions and compensation payments, and it also espouses regime change. Orend concludes that justice after war requires a new Geneva Convention that commits the international community to the construction of "minimally just" regimes that are peaceful, that are legitimate in the view of both their own people and the international community, and that do what they can to satisfy human rights.[63]

Jus post bellum thus breaks with the idea that just wars are limited in their ends by the twin principles of political sovereignty and territorial integrity.[64] Rather, it bolsters the cosmopolitan conception of international order that seeks to ensure the spread of a particular model of human rights across the globe. Moreover, Orend's is what Mark Evans calls a "restricted" conception of jus post bellum because it limits its concerns to the immediate aftermath of war, whereas more expansionist views require further changes to the international order.[65] Nonetheless, either conception of jus post bellum marks a significant break with the traditional theory of just war by limiting the political sovereignty of states and connecting military ethics to questions of domestic justice.[66] Put differently, rather than trying to restrain states, jus post bellum seeks to break the cycle of violence, and promote a world in which rights are more uniformly respected.[67] In other words, it conceives of just wars as a sort of global law enforcement in pursuit of a cosmopolitan, rights protecting order. It thus furthers the project of the advocates of humanitarian intervention and anticipates, as we shall see below, the new revisionism. While it does not yet reject the notion of the moral equality of soldiers, it does display the same universality that traditional just-war theorists bemoan as lacking attention to context.[68] That is the hallmark of the new directions in just-war theory with which we are concerned.

Vignette 2: Justice After War

Regime Change and the Promotion of Democracy: Human Rights and Security in Post-War Reconstruction

Traditional just-war theory stipulates that nations have a right to self-determination and sovereignty, and therefore holds that, following the cessation of war, the victor should seek to restore the previous status quo, although it accepts the necessity of taking steps to remove the situation that led to conflict in the first place. By contrast, cosmopolitan approaches see war as a form of global law enforcement and advocate the development of liberal regimes that do what they can to satisfy human rights. Therefore, the two approaches are radically at odds over questions of regime change and rehabilitation.

For example, the traditional approach would have forbidden the 2003 invasion of Iraq insofar as the goal was the overthrow of the Ba'athist regime and the replacement of Saddam Hussein with something resembling a liberal democracy. While the question of weapons of mass destruction complicates matters somewhat for the traditional view, most exponents of it advocated the continuation and enhancing of inspections and the no-fly zone. On this view, preventive war is illegitimate, and states must actually do something that violates the rights of another state before they lose their own rights to territorial integrity and political sovereignty.

By contrast, so long as they satisfy the other requirements of just war, wars of regime change can be proportional and legitimate on the cosmopolitan approach. Because this approach tries to break the cycle of violence and promote a world in which rights are respected, the internal actions of states can constitute a just cause for war as surely as can violations of the sovereignty of a third party. Moreover, regime change can be a legitimate goal of a war sparked by an external act of aggression, and some cosmopolitans advocated the toppling of Saddam's regime after the first Gulf war of 1991.

In other words, the two approaches to just-war theory differ radically in their assessment of the tasks of post-war reconstruction. Whereas the priority of the traditional theory is to improve the security of the international order, cosmopolitan approaches seek to limit sovereignty so as to promote a more just world order. In practice, it may sometimes be possible to attempt to combine the approaches and to aim at the best of both possible worlds by seeking the establishment of pluralistic institutions, including power-sharing agreements and the separation of powers. However, one of the grave dangers for military forces is being perceived as acting as proxies of imperial powers, in particular when engaged in action in parts of the world with vastly differing norms to those of North America and Western Europe.[69]

REVISIONIST JUST-WAR THEORY

The most important theoretical development in recent military ethics, and that with the most radical implications, is the revisionist approach that holds that the moral distinction between jus ad bellum and jus in bello must be revised such that combatants are held responsible for fighting for an unjust cause, and not merely for particular acts of war. Although at first glance, this argument might seem to be at odds with the claims that the categories of just-war theory need to expand to incorporate jus post bellum, in analyzing these arguments, it is best to understand them as adopting similar theoretical approaches and conceiving of just wars as forms of law making. In assessing the implications of the approach, it is important to highlight the call for the development or strengthening of global institutions designed to judge the justice of particular wars or state arrangements. In other words, the central point of departure shared by the two arguments is that the legalist paradigm needs revision. In the case of revisionist theory, this leads to the claims that the dualism between jus ad bellum and jus in bello must be collapsed, as combatants are not entitled to accept the state's authority when assessing whether the cause for which they fight is just. In considering this argument, we will mostly focus on the approaches of David Rodin and Jeff McMahan, the two most important revisionists.

We should note at the outset that in important ways Walzer anticipated the new revisionism by requiring more of combatants than had previous versions of just-war theory. Most importantly, he revised the "Doctrine of Double Effect" by insisting that soldiers accept risks to themselves in order to minimize those that they impose on civilians.[70] Walzer argued that it was not sufficient for combatants to claim that, while they foresaw that certain military actions would lead to civilian casualties, they did not intend those casualties. Rather, soldiers owe civilians a duty of due care. For example, Walzer suggests that soldiers in World War I who bombed dugouts owed it to potential civilians trapped in the dugouts to shout a warning before throwing the bombs inside.[71] Walzer thus opens the door for the suggestion that soldiers must accept risks for the sake of the morally innocent.

Revisionist just-war theory holds that Walzer does not go far enough in this regard. The starting point for their argument is the claim that while traditional just-war theory and the laws of war, enshrined in the Charter of the United Nations (UN), both suggest that just wars are defensive ones, the argument for self-defense does not work in the same way in the case of war as it does in the case of interpersonal morality.[72] In criminal law, for someone to claim self-defense as a justification when harming another person, the person harmed must have done something to render them liable to attack or the person invoking the claim must be able to claim a lesser-evil justification. In other words, the law conceives of people as being immune from harm unless they do something to lose that immunity or there is an urgent justification akin to Walzer's argument that states may violate principles of jus in bello in cases of supreme emergency.

However, just-war theorists such as Walzer take soldiers to become liable to attack by fighting in war, even if they are prosecuting a just cause. As McMahan notes, committing justified harm would not render someone liable to defensive harm in civil law. The argument that combatants become liable to attack simply by fighting is at odds with principles of personal self-defense. If "a murderer is in the process of killing a number of innocent people and the only way to stop him is to kill him, the police officer who takes aim . . . does not thereby make herself morally liable to defensive action."[73] Rodin makes a similar point, asking, "How does the Just War Theorist get from a right of national-defense held against a state to a right to kill held against a particular person?"[74] In other words, in the traditional argument that grounds state rights in a domestic analogy with individual rights, the rights of individuals are transformed into state rights and so, in effect, states become individuals for the purposes of international law. This means that just-war theory generally assumes that soldiers are liable to attack simply by virtue of posing a threat to other human beings. However, revisionist just-war theorists insist that liability to harm requires moral, not merely causal, responsibility for a threat of harm. In other words, the threat in question must be illegitimate.[75] However, soldiers prosecuting a just war are not morally responsible for an illegitimate threat. As a result, such combatants are not liable to attack. Revisionists thus conclude that, although just-war literature has usually used the term "innocence" as a synonym for "not engaged in harming," in fact, it ought to be used in its ordinary, moral sense as meaning "not guilty of illegitimate acts of harm."[76] In this view, as we shall see, combatants prosecuting an unjust cause are guilty of illegitimate acts of harm; even if they are misled by their government into thinking their war is just.

Put differently, the revisionist argument proceeds from the view that killing in defense of an unjust cause is, morally speaking, killing the innocent and is therefore tantamount to murder. That is why revisionists argue that the traditional distinction between jus ad bellum and jus in bello cannot hold, and soldiers must assess the justice of their army's cause. By contrast, killing in prosecution of a just cause is legitimate, provided, that is, that such killing is both necessary to advance the war's aims and proportionate to them. Aware that this conclusion is somewhat counterintuitive to most, revisionists have advanced defenses of it against many of the most likely objections. The following discussion considers three of the more important of these.[77]

First, revisionists have argued against the view that the moral equality of soldiers can be defended by virtue of the duties of the office itself. This argument sometimes proceeds via an analogy between combatants and prison guards. Like combatants, guards are expected to carry out sentences regardless of any misgivings they have about the justice of the sentence. The reason for that, revisionists argue, is that we assume that the legal system in which the guard works is generally just and grant the excuse if and only if there is good reason to think that it is. Absolute certainty may not be required morally prior to action that would cause harm, but we expect those inflicting such harm to have a strong degree of confidence in the justice of their action. In war, however, this is impossible, because contemporary just-war theory stipulates that no war can be just on both sides and because many wars are unjust on both sides. The upshot is, the revisionists argue, that soldiers cannot presume their war to be just because it is more likely to be unjust.[78] Now, if we were to doubt the fact that domestic legal systems are just, this would not uproot the revisionist argument in and of itself, because the obvious response would be that in cases of injustice, prison guards also have strong reason to doubt whether to impose sentences. The revisionist argument that all combatants should believe that their cause is more likely to be unjust than just may be overstated, but at the very least the argument should call into question the claim that combatants may simply defer moral decision-making to their government.

Second, revisionists argue that the appeal to moral equality makes a conceptual error by confusing the legal categories of "excuse" and "justification." In criminal law, a justification exculpates someone completely because it suggests that an action that would have been wrong in most circumstances is not wrong in the conditions in which it was committed. By contrast, an excuse provides partial diminution of responsibility, but some wrongdoing remains.[79] Revisionists claim that the sorts of arguments that Walzer adduces to support the position that soldiers do not commit a crime if they fight for an unjust cause are presented as though they justified such action, when the considerations that he presents are, at best, excuses. In particular, Walzer's argument that soldiers are moral equals because they are coerced by their states into fighting is, they argue, in effect a claim of duress, which is an excusing condition, not a justification.[80] Combatants coerced by their government are in a position analogous to someone coerced by a criminal into harming a third party. While we might hold that the third party bore most of the responsibility for the harm, generally speaking, we would not regard such duress as justifying but merely excusing the coerced party's actions. Duress does, on this view, excuse not only conscripted soldiers, who are formally coerced, but also those who enlist in order to escape poverty or because dictatorial governments threaten their families. We should perhaps add that it also applies to those who wish to serve their country, if they have good reason to believe that their country generally acts in a just manner and serves as a force for good in the world. However, duress should be considered only a partial excuse, because the possibility of either evading the order or accepting punishment exists and, given the harm that fighting in an unjust war causes, ought to be seriously contemplated by coerced combatants.[81]

Third, and most important, revisionists deny the claim that combatants may legitimately defer to their government's view for epistemic reasons. In the traditional view, it is impossible for soldiers to discern whether a war is just because of lack of information. We saw earlier that Walzer, in defending the moral equality of soldiers, argued that combatants are most likely to trust official propaganda and so believe that their war effort is just.[82] Traditional just-war theorists tend to believe that the ignorance of soldiers about the justice of their side's cause is, in a sense, invincible. That is to say, given a government's influence over the information presented to the public and to the military, it may not be possible for soldiers to uncover the truth. Acknowledging this, McMahan claims that military organizations also deliberately tend to limit the ability of combatants to reflect on the content of their orders and to offer scarcely any education on the morality of war.[83] Moreover, that which they do provide misleads combatants into believing that, even if their cause is unjust, it is permissible for them to participate in it.[84] It is important not to accept McMahan's claims uncritically; many military forces around the world, including the U.S. military, do devote great attention to just-war theory. However, they tend to teach the doctrine of the moral equality of soldiers and to underemphasize critical reflection on jus ad bellum and in particular on the requirement of just cause. In particular, traditional just-war theory, which remains the dominant focus of the military, concludes that, if wrong is indeed done when soldiers fight in an unjust war, the responsibility lies with the government, and perhaps with military leaders, and not with ordinary combatants. That is because combatants believe their cause is just and could not believe otherwise, given both the paucity of information and the social and cultural pressures to accept government authority. Moreover, even if combatants do doubt the justice of their country's war, they are not given an opportunity to act on that doubt.

Revisionist just-war theory denies that these considerations amount to a legitimate justification for combatants to accept the call to fight, given the considerations adduced earlier about the likelihood of a war being unjust. McMahan devotes the most attention to this argument, and concludes that a particular soldier's decision whether to fight may make little difference from the point of view of consequences.[85] Someone else would fight in her place if she refused to fight. There are two sorts of moral risks increased if she fights and that should therefore persuade her not to do so.[86] The first is that, morally speaking, there is an important difference between actively doing something and allowing it to happen. It is, McMahan holds, "more seriously wrong to kill innocent people . . . than it is to allow innocent people to be killed." So a soldier who, not knowing whether his side's war is just or not, accepts the order to fight and goes on to kill innocent people does a greater wrong than does the one who refuses the order to fight and so allows innocents to die.[87] Second, the confluence of the facts that most wars are actually unjust and that most combatants believe their wars to be just should, McMahan argues, encourage considerable skepticism about the justice of a particular war and encourage us to err on the side of caution because of "the natural bias in favor of believing that one is right."[88] In other words, because we tend to be inclined to believe that the wars our country fights are just and yet know that most wars are unjust, in cases of uncertainty, "the presumption should be that the morally safer course is not to fight."[89] However, as discussed later, it should also be noted that the abstraction of the foregoing argument ignores the fact that states may have differential histories of justice in war. As McMahan notes, it would be less risky for a soldier from Norway to accept her government's verdict than for one from the United States to do so, because Norway does not have the same history of fighting unjust wars as that of the United States.[90]

The upshot of these arguments is that, according to the revisionists, soldiers are not moral equals and cannot defer to their government's authority when deciding whether a particular war is legitimate. As soldiers who are fighting in defense of a just cause have done nothing to render themselves liable to attack, to kill them would be morally equivalent to an act of murder. Rodin asks rhetorically, "how can soldiers whose very war is unjust be engaged in an activity for which they are free of fault?"[91] His answer, which is reminiscent of the arguments advanced by the advocates of jus post bellum discussed in the previous section, is that there is a tension at the heart of just-war theory between jus ad bellum, which aims to restrain states from fighting wars, and jus in bello, which aims to make war a rule-governed activity.[92] On this view, leaving jus ad bellum as the responsibility of political leaders allows too great a degree of statism into our thinking about military ethics, and a more thoroughgoing individualism would require us to treat soldiers as moral agents and not merely as victims of government coercion.[93]

When assessing the revisionist approach, we shall consider whether the impossibility of applying such an individualism universally ought to give us pause, as well as consider the radical implications of this argument for the practice of modern warfare in posing a stark challenge to the disciplinary techniques of military training. However, it is worth first considering one of the theoretical complexities, namely that the revisionist argument may also undermine the central principle of jus in bello, non-combatant immunity. McMahan notes early on in *Killing in War* that it is a mistake to equate "discrimination" and "non-combatant immunity," because the distinction between legitimate and illegitimate targets may not map on neatly to that between combatants and non-combatants.[94] This is because, on his version of the liability model, moral responsibility for an illegitimate threat or harm may render someone liable to attack.[95] Given that some civilians bear such responsibility for illegitimate threats, some civilians may be liable to attack, provided this would avert the harm.

To show that situations do arise in which civilians bear moral responsibility for an illegitimate threat, McMahan considers the case of the American invasion of Guatemala in 1954. Accepting McMahan's description of the situation for the sake of argument, this involved the forcible overthrow of a democratically elected government and its replacement by a series of military juntas.[96] One major cause of the invasion was the pressure that the senior executives of the United Fruit Company, who objected to Guatemalan President Jacobo Arbenz Guzman's nationalization of United Fruit Company property, exerted on the Dwight Eisenhower government. McMahan invites us to consider whether it would have been legitimate for the Guatemalan Army to prevent the coup by assassinating the executives of the United Fruit Company if doing so would have had a realistic chance of success. He suggests that it would have because the executives had rendered themselves liable to attack "by their role in instigating an unjust war."[97] McMahan adds that such an action might even have been preferable to waging a regular war—even if they were somehow successful against the might of the U.S. Army—because the Guatemalan soldiers who would have been killed in such a war had not committed a moral wrong. McMahan concludes that the principle of non-combatant immunity must give way to a principle of discrimination based on moral responsibility for harm rather than the posing of harm.

However, it would be a mistake to think that revisionist just-war theory simply does away with the principle of non-combatant immunity. McMahan immediately qualifies his claim about the United Fruit Company by noting how rare it is for civilians to be able to influence government policy to such an extent and adding that it is "fanciful and contrived" to imagine that killing the executives might have averted the threat to the Guatemalan Government.[98] Moreover, he adds that the moral immunity of civilians, for the most part, can be arrived at by considering the combined force of different factors, such as lack of responsibility, ineffectiveness, and the commingling of innocent and responsible civilians.[99] In addition, he insists that his arguments do not offer support for terrorist attacks that pay lip service to ideas of moral responsibility. Most importantly, he insists that "pragmatic considerations argue decisively for an absolute, exceptionless legal prohibition of intentional military attacks against civilians," and suggests that this is a place where the morality of war must separate from the laws of war.[100] However, bearing in mind that McMahan's analysis suggests that responsible civilians are more liable to attack than are just combatants, we might consider whether his arguments open the door to attacks on civilians in counterinsurgent operations in which civilians are often active participants.

Perhaps for this reason, other revisionists reject McMahan's argument about non-combatant immunity altogether. Notably, Rodin argues for what he calls "restrictive asymmetry"; that is, for the position that, while unjust combatants should have fewer privileges in war than granted by the war convention, just warriors should have the same duties as hitherto and should be expected to comply with the extant principles of jus in bello.[101] As noted earlier, this is the type of asymmetry that Walzer fails to consider in *Just and Unjust Wars*. His discussion of the sliding scale rejects the view that those fighting for a just cause should have more privileges than unjust warriors should so that they are entitled to violate principles of jus in bello. However, this is the possibility that Rodin calls "permissive asymmetry." By contrast, Rodin's variant of the sliding scale would not allow just warriors to violate jus in bello but would deny unjust ones any war rights at all.

In short, Rodin argues that, while unjust warriors should be held accountable for fighting for an unjust cause, this does not mean that just warriors may target civilians, even if those civilians are morally responsible for an illegitimate threat. Rather, he holds, the liability model, if properly used, restricts war rights of soldiers to those fighting for a just cause and refuses to grant anyone else the right to harm anyone in war. The thesis underlying Rodin's work is that human rights apply everywhere and do not cease to exist on the edge of the battlefield. In practice, McMahan concurs with this position in almost all circumstances. The hard core of the revisionist principle is, then, that the distinction between jus ad bellum and jus in bello does not hold. Soldiers are not morally equal, because those defending a just cause harm only those who are liable to harm, while those fighting for an unjust cause harm the morally innocent and thus commit serious injustice. The principles of jus in bello may be what traditional just-war theory has taken them to be, but in this approach, they depend on the prior satisfaction of jus ad bellum, and in particular of the requirement of just cause. As this approach denies states the sovereign right to wage war for reasons of their own and seeks to reconstitute the international order such that recourse to war is limited, we understand it best if we build on the earlier cosmopolitan approaches and seek to replace war with international police work.[102]

Vignette 3: Revisionist Just-War Theory

Non-Combatant Immunity: The Case of the United Fruit Company Executives and the Coup in Guatemala (Or the Forcible Overthrow of a Democratic Regime for Reasons of Realpolitik)

As mentioned previously, the most radical implication of the revisionist approach to just-war theory is that, in some versions of it, it may undercut the jus in bello principle of non-combatant immunity. Given that this is probably the most widely accepted principle of just war theory in the public imagination, it is worth considering further.

According to the revisionist argument, the moral basis for liability to attack in war is being morally responsible for an unjustified threat of harm. Absent such a threat, people are immune to such harm. However, it is clearly the case that there can be circumstances in which people whom we would ordinarily consider civilians are morally responsible for an unjustified threat. Consider, for example, the American invasion of Guatemala in 1954, discussed in the text. If the description offered there does not satisfy, consider a hypothetical version of it tailored to fit the description: because of pressure exerted by a major international corporation that wishes to gain access to foreign markets, a powerful democratic country is considering

31

going to war with a far less powerful but democratic country in its sphere of influence. Although the powerful state is committed to democratic governing, both at home and abroad, it has pledged to maintain its sphere of influence to resist the encroachment of a hostile foreign power pledged to overthrow the political system of the powerful democracy. Unfortunately for the less-powerful country, it is in this sphere of influence and its democratically-elected government bears a resemblance—but only a passing one—to that of the hostile foreign power. It is, in fact, a legitimate government that is not under the influence of the foreign power, but the international corporation is able to exploit the fear of that foreign power in the minds of the leaders of the powerful democracy, and there is a real risk of invasion.

What should the small democracy do? According to traditional just-war theory, its only legitimate recourse is a war of national defense. However, given that it is hopelessly outmatched militarily, even that would be ruled out by the jus ad bellum requirement that wars have a reasonable hope of success. While it could appeal to international assistance, this is unlikely to be forthcoming because of the might of the neighboring power and the lack of strategic significance of our benighted small democracy. It would seem as though surrender and negotiation is its only option.

In this instance, however, some versions of revisionist just-war theory present it with another option. It could attempt to assassinate the chief executives of the international corporation. This strategy might work because the intelligence agencies of the small democracy are sufficient to carry out the task effectively and because, with the chief executives out of the way, the powerful democracy might stay its hand and not carry out the invasion. The targeted assassinations would therefore fulfill the requirement of reasonable hope of success. Furthermore, they would be morally preferable to war because the chief executives have acted in ways that render them liable to attack, whereas the soldiers of the small democracy who would be killed in the defensive war have not acted so.

What should militaries do in such circumstances? The moral stigma on attacking non-combatants is high, and rightfully so. Indeed, some revisionists insist that non-combatants may indeed never be attacked, and even McMahan, who dissents from this view, believes that all such attacks should be **legally**, if not morally, prohibited. However, insofar as non-combatant immunity rests on the moral status of those rendered invulnerable, it is worth reconsidering the question of whether we should indeed regard all non-combatants, in all times and places, as innocent in the relevant respects.

ASSESSMENT

To some, revisionist just-war theory will look, as McMahan admits, "plainly crazy,"[103] like "moral theory gone mad, the recommendations of [theorists] without the slightest sense of realism."[104] However, as advocates of the traditional approach now recognize, the majority of philosophers today accept its critique of the moral equality of soldiers.[105] The following text provides an account of the importance of the revisionist approach to the theory and practice of contemporary warfare, and will try to explain this curious fact. The importance of the revisionist argument lies in the confluence of three factors. Taken together, they suggest, as argued in the next section, the need for significant changes to military practice, even though some of the changes should be reactions against revisionism.

The first feature of the revisionist argument that makes it worthy of our attention is that it is best understood as part of a broader cosmopolitan approach to just-war theory that seeks to strengthen international institutions to reduce the incidence of war and ensure greater protection of human rights before, during, and after war. This is the direction in which just-war theory has been moving steadily for several decades, and it offers the possibility of transforming the world order, while ensuring greater compliance with emerging international norms related to the legitimate use of force and the responsibility to protect. While earlier forms of the cosmopolitan argument had tended to focus their attention on limiting the political sovereignty of nation-states that traditional just-war theory upholds, revisionism attempts to extend the concern with raising the moral requirements of war to individual combatants. As noted, this was a feature of Walzer's secularized version of traditional just-war theory, which requires soldiers to take risks in order to protect non-combatants, regardless of their nationality. Even if we are skeptical about the possibilities of global transformation or adopt a more positive attitude toward the state than do cosmopolitans, the attempt to use just-war theory to reduce the incidence of violence and encourage greater moral thought on the part of individual combatants is important. It should prompt militaries to incorporate a greater focus on jus ad bellum in their education on just-war theory.

Second, cosmopolitan approaches are a natural product of deploying the techniques of analytic philosophy to the question of just-war theory. As evidence of this, it is worth noting that Robert Nozick had suggested that combatants must judge the justice of their army's cause as early as the 1970s, before Walzer wrote

Just and Unjust Wars. Nozick claimed that, "It is a soldier's responsibility to determine if his side's cause is just; if he finds the issue tangled, unclear, or confusing, he may not shift the responsibility to his leaders."[106] Likewise, Orend has argued that at least some combatants ought to refuse to participate in war because they know or should know that it is unjust, and that if they do not do so, they are "like minor accomplices to a major crime."[107] What is new about the revisionist approach is its emphasis on the argument that combatants must make individual decisions about the justice of the cause for which they are called to fight, not the argument itself.

What makes the argument a likely outcome of deploying the methods of analytic philosophy to the ethics of war is the abstraction and universalism of those methods, which encourage theorists to adopt a relatively a-contextual attitude toward moral questions and to treat military ethics as continuous with all other aspects of personal morality. Nozick's account of the methods he uses is particularly instructive. There are, he says, "elaborate arguments, claims rebutted by unlikely counterexamples, surprising theses, puzzles, abstract structural conditions, challenges to find another theory which fits a specified range of cases, startling conclusions," and so on.[108] McMahan and Rodin tend to be somewhat more interested in the context of war than that, but the liability model that is at the heart of their approach also assumes that there is nothing particular about war that might make the principles appropriate to it discontinuous with those of interpersonal relations.

By contrast, Walzer's argument for the moral equality of soldiers rests on one of the characteristic crutches of his theory: that war cannot be understood by analogy with activities in civil society and, in particular, that we cannot ground military ethics in a comparison with the principles of individual self-defense.[109] A bank robber who kills a bank guard has no right to claim that she acted in self-defense because she was responsible for robbing the bank in the first place. By contrast, soldiers are not responsible for the wars in which they fight and so should not be treated as invoking a claim of self-defense in a conflict that they started. That is why they are not, in Walzer's account, criminals when they kill enemy soldiers.[110] The absence of responsibility for the conflict makes the situation of soldiers different from that of bank robbers. More generally, war is distinctive, Walzer argues, for three reasons. First, it is an intensely coercive experience, and is so in "ways that are probably not equaled anywhere else."[111] Second, it is "an intensely collective and collectivizing experience" which attempts to treat individual actions, that are fraught with difficulty, separately.[112] Finally, it is "a world of radical and pervasive uncertainty,"[113] such that assessments of moral risk are almost impossible. Requiring them would make almost any action whatsoever impossible. As a result, Walzer concludes, "wars and battles are not 'cases' to which the law and morality of everyday life can be applied," but activities that represent a radical break from the social round and so must be treated on their own merits.[114]

In short, both the new revisionism, and the cosmopolitan just-war theory of which it is a part, are important not only because of the issues they raise but also because of the question of approach that they ought to prompt. If we want to challenge the idea that soldiers must judge the justice of their side's cause, we will have to insist that military ethics are a form of role morality and reject the idea that we can develop useful principles of just war by virtue of an analogy with non-military activity. Rather, just-war theorists would have to focus on the history and practice of warfare.[115] They would also need to pay careful attention to the implications of their arguments for democratic theory and practice, and in particular, to be at pains not to undermine the principle that military forces must be subordinated to civilian oversight so that the Armed Forces are the servant of the public, not its master. However, this argument for the particularism of just-war theory might be more radical than Walzer himself recognizes, for his justification of the rights of states is grounded in what he labels the "domestic analogy" with individual rights,[116] and so might not survive the move to treating just-war theory as a specific role morality.

The third reason why the revisionist argument is important, is moral. Its insistence that, regardless of the circumstances of war, taking a life remains one of the, if not the, gravest things we can do to another person and is a major contribution to the theory. It is the moral intuition underlying and guiding McMahan's work in particular, and it explains the power of any theorist's attempt to restrain and limit recourse to war.[117] Thus, one of the great benefits of revisionist just-war theory is that it pushes us to do more to try to hold armies accountable for taking lives by insisting that the defense of following superior orders does not justify the waging of aggressive war and only partially excuses it. If we insist on recourse for armies as institutions to incorporate the possibility of selective conscientious objection to particular wars, we may prevent unnecessary destruction. This is particularly so because the experience of many just-war theorists in recent decades has been that officers of the Armed

Forces tend to be less bellicose and more concerned for the ethics of their conduct than are their civilian leaders.[118]

In other words, the revisionists are right to argue that the doctrine of the moral equality of soldiers needs rethinking, because it enables soldiers to side-step the moral question of whether the taking of life is justified. Granting combatants carte blanche to fight without considering why they fight makes the decision too unreflective, and holding soldiers morally accountable for their actions in war does not make up for this. However, this does not necessarily mean that combatants should have to make individual decisions about whether to take up arms. A preferable conclusion might be that military forces should allow combatants to object conscientiously, or at least to rethink their policy on dishonorable discharge, without branding combatants who obey the democratic order to fight as murderers.

Vignette 4: Assessment

Selective Conscientious Objection

When should a soldier be permitted to refuse to fight in a particular war? Can militaries accept continued service from those who do so? These are questions on which both types of just-war theory offer different answers and where military practice diverges yet again.

Imagine the following scenario: a mid-ranking officer has a distinguished record of service, having been on tours of duty in multiple combat zones over the course of more than a decade, and having fought bravely throughout. She has only ever questioned one order, and that one turned out to be an illegal order that would have violated the principles of jus in bello by firing on civilians. Our officer, then, has repeatedly demonstrated her loyalty to both her country and its Armed Forces and the laws of war enshrined in the Geneva Conventions.

Now, however, the country is about to embark on war with a state that may be harboring terrorists but that claims to be doing all it can to root out the cells itself. If the war goes ahead, many civilians will die. The officer refuses to serve, saying that she is committed to the views that the only legitimate military action is clearly defensive, and that the counterterrorism operation can proceed just as effectively by means of intelligence work involving force short of war but not a full-scale war. She insists that she will disobey all orders relating to the war and is willing to face court-martial and dishonorable discharge, although she reiterates her patriotism and willingness to abide by any orders that she takes to be legal.

What should be done? On the one hand, if the officer is allowed to continue to serve, this may encourage future acts of disobedience that would render military discipline impossible. On the other, her previous refusal to obey a jus in bello order did not have this effect. Revisionist just-war theory encourages Armed Forces to search for means of incorporating selective conscientious objection or at least to rethink the policy on dishonorable discharge. In combination with its argument for further development of cosmopolitan institutions, perhaps such accommodation can be found, but in the meantime, this remains a pressing issue for contemporary military practice.

IMPLICATIONS

If we adopt an ambivalent attitude toward revisionist just-war theory, we will nonetheless have to recognize that the implications for both the theory and the practice of contemporary warfare are radical almost to the point of being revolutionary. Given the underlying conceptualization of just wars as forms of international law enforcement, a view that is premised on rejection of the political sovereignty of nation-states, the first major implication is for extending the remit of global institutions such as the International Criminal Court, such that they can make rulings on jus ad bellum war crimes. In other words, international consideration of the decision by states to resort to war may be a useful implication of the claim that states do not have the sovereign prerogative to resort to war for reasons of state. Second, given the challenge to military discipline that the revisionist approach suggests, there is a need to incorporate revisionist just-war theory within military ethics education, and more focus is needed on just cause as it relates to particular wars. Related to this, this author calls for a rethinking of the policy on conscientious objection or at least of dishonorable discharge. Finally, there is a need within just-war theory for greater debate about methods, so as to consider the nature of combatant duties as a form of role morality and to recognize the continuity of just-war theory not only with social justice, as cosmopolitans advocate, but also with collective decision-making problems and, thus, with democratic theory.

The Need to Strengthen Global Legal Institutions

Cosmopolitan approaches to just-war theory tend to conceptualize just wars as forms of global law enforcement and thus to dream of a world in which combatants operate more like police officers than soldiers. It will come as no surprise that revisionist just-war theorists have also called for strengthening global institutions to reduce the political sovereignty of nation-states. They come to this argument because they tend to shy away from suggesting that ordinary combatants should receive legal punishment for participating in unjust wars, in part because of the logistical and motivational difficulties that trying large numbers of soldiers would cause, but also because of the mitigating excuses that apply to most of them. Of particular importance as an excuse is the epistemic problem discussed above: namely, that because of government propaganda, misinformation, and classification of relevant material, it is often impossible for soldiers to know the relevant details of the circumstances surrounding the military buildup to war. Revisionists such as McMahan argue that, in cases of uncertainty, it is less risky to fight than not to fight, but they recognize that the epistemic problem means that there are moral risks regardless of which choice a combatant makes. As a result, revisionist just-war theory often incorporates a divergence between the morality and the law of war.[119]

In an attempt to mitigate this problem, McMahan has recently called for the establishment of an ad bellum branch of the International Criminal Court. This court could "codify our understanding of jus ad bellum in a body of deontic principles stating prohibitions, permissions, and perhaps requirements concerning the resort to war" and rule on whether particular wars cohere with those principles.[120] Similarly, Rodin suggests that, while we should not view just wars as a form of punishment or law enforcement undertaken by particular states, a model of legitimate international law enforcement is possible. It would require "a body which was genuinely impartial and which had a recognized authority to resolve disputes and enforce the law," which would undertake military action to prevent aggression and punish those responsible for it.[121] Rodin thus takes the argument for international institutions a step further than McMahan, suggesting the possibility of a world state and rejecting the traditional philosophical arguments advanced by cosmopolitans such as Kant against such a state.[122]

A world state might seem to be the ultimate implication of cosmopolitan just-war approaches, but it is, obviously, not a possibility in the near future, so it will not be considered further. What, however, of McMahan's suggestion of an international court to rule on the justice of resort to war? In its favor, McMahan holds that such a court might extricate soldiers from their predicament, as well as help to bolster the jus ad bellum requirement of "legitimate authority."[123] While as fallible as any other human institution, such a court would produce judgments with "a stronger claim to epistemic reliability than the pronouncements of warring states, which are inevitably lacking in impartiality and disinterestedness."[124] There are, of course, political problems in getting countries to sign onto such a court, as well as questions about the setup of the court. If the court were constituted in such a way that it did little more than serve the interests of powerful states looking for a warrant to act overseas for reasons of state, in fact, it might cloud the epistemic issue further by lending an aura of impartiality to what were in reality the interests of a strong aggressor state, at the expense of its weaker victims. However, at the level of principle, there would be potential advantages to such a court. Epistemically speaking, as Walzer acknowledges, such a court would make soldiers more like the bank robbers that McMahan's analysis compares them to, because they would now know that there was a judgment ruling that their activity was wrong.[125] While it is unlikely that such rulings could deter warring states, McMahan plausibly argues that some combatants might be more reluctant to fight in light of a judgment that the war their army was about to wage was unjust and that civilians might stop supporting the war or even start to oppose it.[126] Furthermore, especially if military forces allow selective conscientious objection in cases where the court has ruled the war unjust, it might well be that civilian leaders would be less likely to resort to war in such cases because of the danger of widespread disobedience. Thus, the court might mitigate the need for combatants to object to their country's cause. In effect, a court ruling that a war is just would strengthen military discipline.

On the other hand, short of a general transformation of international politics such that a world state emerges, such a court could never be anything more than advisory. The obvious reasons for this have to do with political feasibility. States are highly unlikely to sign over their war-making powers to an international court and equally unlikely to sign on to a court that could order the prosecution of combatants from the state's military forces. However, the more fundamental reasons are principled ones. States should not sign on to such a court and combatants should not sign over their deliberative autonomy to it. In other words, an international court would need to sit alongside the self-determination of (at least) democratic states, while it could only ameliorate and not resolve the epistemic problems of judging the case for going to war.[127] The following paragraphs will discuss a little about each of these two things in turn.

First, the court might downplay the moral desirability of the current regime of self-help, which rests on the value of political participation in moral decision-making.[128] Yitzhak Benbaji has made this argument in terms of accountability, arguing that McMahan's court would need to be accountable not merely to those immediately affected by its rulings, but also to outsiders.[129] The reason is, as Benbaji points out, the moral task when considering the design of the international system is not how to prevent all wars but how to balance the costs and benefits of different institutional designs. In this case, that means balancing the costs of war against the benefits of self-determination, and so even the desirability of limiting participation in unjust wars does not in and of itself justify the court. As he puts it, "if our interest in fair political participation" is great and if "the risk of an aggressive war, which would be prevented under a different regime" is much smaller, the self-help system may be preferable to the court "despite the fact that it permits obedient armies, and thus puts innocents under the risk of being legally killed by unjust combatants."[130] In other words, the good that an international court might do in restricting states' abilities to fight unjust wars needs to be balanced against the benefits of political regimes fitted to a scale in which people can participate or, at least, with which they can identify. While the urging by lawyers and philosophers of non-participation may be beneficial in that it would increase the public consideration of the morality of war, if the rulings were binding, we would deny institutional space for public disagreement with the court's opinion. Unless the court has a merely advisory role, then it may create a democratic deficit. As Walzer points out, McMahan's court would, in practice, merely appeal to individual consciences, and many of us may feel that, even while we demonstrate against our country's war while at home, we should also participate in it for reasons of solidarity.[131] As the avoidance of war is not the only moral good, institutional design dedicated to reducing the incidence of war needs to proceed with an eye to fostering other important goods, such as that of democratic participation.

Second, the court cannot solve the epistemic problem because it cannot be sure to collect all the information relevant to the casus belli and, more importantly, because lack of information is only one reason for disagreement about whether a war is just. In fact, even where there is full information, disagreement about justice is endemic to moral argument, both about war and about every other normative issue. Even if the court is more reliable than the sovereign states over whom it would sit in judgment, it cannot be perfectly reliable, and individual combatants are going to continue to disagree with it. If combatants may not defer to the authority of others in cases of disagreement as revisionists argue, then they cannot simply defer to the authority of an international court, for the court may turn out to have been mistaken, according to some subsequent ruling. On the revisionists' own terms, then, the court cannot do what McMahan intends it to do, because nobody can make a moral decision that removes all risk from those other people who would defer to it.

However, many people understand moral reasoning in dialogic terms, as something that we do together, sometimes as a democratic unit, but often in smaller groups. On this view, the way out of the problem posed by moral and epistemic uncertainty about the justice of resort to war is not to individualize the decision but to democratize the decision-making process by allowing

45

more widespread participation in the discussion. That is why critiques of revisionist just-war theory tend to appeal to the importance of political participation.[132] In this view, the argument that soldiers are not required to assess for themselves the justice of their army's war does not appeal to "epistemic" limitations or to ignorance. Rather, it holds that democratic decisions are morally preferable because they are produced by public debate and contestation. This does not mean that such decisions are always right or must always be obeyed, but it does enjoin an attitude of humility toward our private judgments. Soldiers can never be sure that they are right and the polity wrong when judging the justice of particular wars. Indeed, McMahan accepts that the distinction between just and unjust combatants is more or less always a simple one of moral luck.[133] In such a situation, courts do not help combatants, who need the security provided by the presence of a collective decision-making process to ameliorate the moral precariousness of their situation. The court may be useful in terms of participation in providing specialist input into the ethical dilemma, but it would need to sit alongside other venues for discussion of the justice of war, which is why it is so important for Armed Forces to incorporate discussion of just cause as an ongoing part of war preparation and planning.

Vignette 5: Strengthening Global Legal Institutions

The Judgment of the International Criminal Court

As discussed in the main text, some revisionist just-war theorists have called for the establishment of an ad bellum branch of the International Criminal Court to adjudicate on the justice of resort to war. While the establishment of such a court might help shed light on some of the murkier aspects of international politics, it might also create thorny new dilemmas for Armed Forces around the world.

For example, imagine that a coalition of countries intends to go to war in defense of a third party that has had its sovereignty violated. However, the territory in question is hotly disputed, with both sides having claimed it as their own for more than a century. In this situation, it is extremely hard to tell which side has a just cause; meanwhile, war is underway and people are dying. For reasons of national security, the coalition is unable to present all of the relevant information at the ad bellum branch of the court, and the judgment goes against it: its war of defense is ruled to be illegal.

What should it do now? Following the ruling, some soldiers are refusing to participate in the war, declaring it an unjust war of aggrandizement and accepting discharge. However, while this would make fighting the war more difficult, it would not be impossible. The coalition remains convinced that the resort to war is justified, but it also believes that the increasing institutionalization of just-war practices is both legitimate and necessary if we are to reduce the incidence of war and promote respect for human rights around the world. Waging war in spite of the court's ruling would jeopardize this latter aim. While a traditional just-war theorist might not consider such a prospect particularly serious, because it conceives of war as an inevitable feature of an international system consisting of states with twin rights to sovereignty and territorial integrity, to the cosmopolitan, this is a major concern.

It is unlikely that there is any rule that could be developed that would resolve this dilemma entirely. The judgment of any international court would have to be advisory, and there might be situations in which states would legitimately ignore its rulings. However, a ruling that a war was illegitimate would be a factor in determining whether a war is just or not, even for a state that is convinced the ruling is wrong. This is because the ruling adds weight to the case against war by virtue of the fact that upholding the war would have advantageous long-term consequences by strengthening the court. When considering whether the war is proportionate or not, the coalition would now have to consider not only the loss of life that war would bring but also the damage to the international court's ability to promote respect for human rights and the laws of war around the world.

The Need for Greater Focus on Jus Ad Bellum within Military Education on Just-War Theory and to Rethink the Policy on Dishonorable Discharge

Revisionist just-war theory raises the moral stakes for combatants by declaring them guilty of a moral wrong if they fight in an unjust war. The clear implication is that they must be allowed to refuse to fight in a war that they deem unjust. McMahan notes this clearly, arguing that, while there may be prima facie duties to defer to the authority of the government and to sustain just institutions, these duties are outweighed by the more basic moral duty of avoiding killing innocent human beings.[134] While revisionists often shy away from arguing that soldiers should be punished for fighting in an unjust war, they nonetheless hold that the appropriate moral response to an order to fight in war is to consider for oneself whether that war is just. Given that the moral intuition underlying revisionism—that taking a life is a matter of the gravest concern—insistence on deliberation about a war's ends seems sound, even if we shy away from concurring with revisionists that the actual decision-making must be individual. However, many combatants are not equipped to think about, or participate in, a discussion of the ethics of war. Moreover, bearing in mind that militaries around the world believe themselves to rely on a rigid, hierarchical chain of command in order to function effectively, the barriers to incorporation of discussion of the revisionist perspective are high.

Nonetheless, the effort is worth making. The positive benefit of focus on jus ad bellum within institutional fora such as education programs is that it would help to reduce the isolation of soldiers who doubt the justice of their country's cause. Moreover, it may be that an army that drags its soldiers to war unwillingly is, in fact, a less cohesive unit than one confident in the commitment of its soldiers. In so far as that commitment depends on the soldiers recognizing the justice of what they are fighting for, institutional focus on just cause may lead to greater, not lesser, military effectiveness. Put differently, if discipline is crucial to the ability to fight well, then just-war theory is an important part of military training because it inculcates discipline by making combatants aware of the harm that they cause if they do not fight with respect for moral limits. Moreover, as Walzer pointed out at the start of *Just and Unjust Wars*, the language of morality is in important ways analogous with that of strategy, which suggests that there are strategic benefits wrought by ethics education.[135]

On the other hand, if we teach that an approach to just-war theory encourages soldiers to disobey orders that they deem unjust, there is an obvious sense in which it may jeopardize military discipline. However, it is worth bearing in mind that not only the orthodox morality of war but also the laws of war allow, and in fact require, soldiers to disobey illegal military orders; that is, those which mandate a jus in bello violation.[136] Indeed, even in the heat of battle, many soldiers do refuse to obey orders to fire at civilians, often accepting great risks to themselves, including the risk of punishment, in order to avoid killing non-combatants.[137] Yet such refusal is not widely thought to make military discipline impossible. Indeed, it could be argued that training soldiers to obey all orders except for those that require them to commit a war crime is to prepare them for a more reflexive discipline that internalizes the moral and legal requirements of justice in war. Moreover, as McMahan points out, provisions for conscientious disobedience to jus ad bellum orders would likely be less disruptive than those for jus in bello ones, because of the diminished capacity for rational deliberation on the battlefield.[138] Were institutional provisions made available for soldiers to object conscientiously to particular wars as a whole, the less frenzied nature of preparations for battle might make for reasoned moral deliberation that is impossible once combat has begun.

However, one might argue that refusing to participate in a particular war is, in effect, choosing to opt out of the Armed Forces altogether. Whereas in civil society, a conscientious objector can always perform some other sort of civic duty, it would place an intolerable burden on the Armed Forces to expect them to divide tasks such that combatants only worked on campaigns of which they approved. Moreover, combatants receive pay and benefits to be ready when the country calls that they should not receive if they are not ready, particularly because, if large numbers opt out, the army as a whole will be unable to function. While that is a good thing if the selective objection really is conscientious, we can imagine circumstances in which combatants use moral arguments to disguise unwillingness to fight in, say, defense of a third party or in a humanitarian intervention. It is at least worth asking whether a country should send its army to war when sufficient numbers of its soldiers refuse to fight to jeopardize the prospect of prosecuting the war successfully. The problem is the likelihood that wars fought in defense of distant countries might not attract willing soldiers, while unjust wars in which national fervor is aroused by propaganda campaigns are fought willingly.

Whereas on the one hand, selective conscientious objection to particular wars seems analogous to selective conscientious objection to particular orders in battle, on the other hand it may amount in effect to resignation from one's post. An important question for future research, then, should consist in whether it is possible for armies to allow soldiers to object conscientiously or whether such objection should be seen as requiring a discharge, perhaps without honor. However, it certainly appears possible that adverse rulings of an international court could help ameliorate many of these problems by making resort to war less likely because both government and military leaders would know that they would face strong internal resistance to the decision to go to war.

Vignette 6: The Military Curriculum

Teaching Jus Ad Bellum

Because the Armed Forces tend to think of resorting to war as the responsibility of civilian leaders, education programs in the military tend to focus on jus in bello, ensuring that soldiers abide by legal orders on the battlefield but refuse to comply with illegal ones. However, cosmopolitan approaches to just war insist that soldiers are also responsible for assessing the justice of their resort to war by their Armed Forces. This means that military education must focus also on jus ad bellum.

Here, however, there are a few dilemmas for military practice. First, time and resources are limited, and any increase in attention to jus ad bellum would divert them both away from jus in bello. Second, there is a danger of disrupting military discipline. Third, there is the question of what to teach. Most recent just-war theory uses the methods of analytic philosophy and treats military ethics as it would any other branch of applied ethics. On the traditional view, just-war theory is continuous with military practice, and the study of the subject requires focus on the history and practice of warfare. This is even more true for jus ad bellum, because assessing the justice of a particular war requires detailed knowledge of conditions on the ground and the history of the dispute in question.

How should we devise an educational syllabus that meets these conflicting goals? The best approach may be to try to combine the two, teaching both moral philosophy and military history, but this cannot resolve all problems, especially because the two frequently lead to contradictory conclusions. It is important that soldiers be able to think through the implications of different ethical scenarios, and that they be informed about international politics and theory.

This makes the construction of the curriculum for education on just-war theory one of the most pressing requirements of contemporary academia when seeking to ensure that its wars are conducted ethically.

The Need for Debate about Methodological Foundations in Just-War Theory

Throughout this monograph, it is suggested that at stake in the debate between traditional and cosmopolitan or revisionist just-war theory is the approach that is appropriate to military ethics. Whereas the traditional view sees the role of a soldier as taking up a specific morality of its own that is discontinuous with personal morality and that is more closely related to democratic theory, revisionists use the methods of analytic philosophy and treat just-war theory via analogy with interpersonal morality. These different methods lead to rather different conclusions and so suggest a need to try to teach both with military ethics education. This is especially so, bearing in mind the argument that the moral intuition underlying the revisionist argument is sound, and that taking a life should be approached with the utmost care, but that the theory needs to consider the importance of democratic participation. However, choices will sometimes have to be made, for the approaches can lead to conclusions that are not only different, but also often incompatible with each other.

Let us consider that Walzer, the major theoretical advocate of the doctrine of the moral equality of soldiers, had earlier in his career supported the case for selective conscientious objection to particular wars in the context of American involvement in Vietnam.[139] In this view, we can support soldiers' rights both to refuse to fight in wars they deem unjust and to fight in solidarity with their country, even while demonstrating against the war politically. To many revisionists, the suggestion that there is no incompatibility between supporting a soldier's rights to conscientious objection and to obedient participation motivated by solidarity will seem contradictory. In this view, either a war is just or it is unjust. If it is just, soldiers should fight in it. If it is unjust, they should not. This points to the fact that the revisionist approach relies heavily on the idea that moral questions are, if we have sufficient information, susceptible of an objectively right answer.[140] On this account, one of the reasons that jus ad bellum needs to be reworked is that it does not provide the clear guidance that morality ought to provide. Approaching morality in this way implies that we can solve ethical problems by designing appropriately impartial decision procedures and applying them to particular cases, such as that of war.

By contrast, defenses of the notion of the moral equality of soldiers often rest on a view of morality as both intersubjective and socially produced.[141] It is for this reason that Walzer bases his just-war theory on what he calls the "moral reality of war," and not on a priori inquiry using the methods of analytic philosophy. That is to say, what gives the principle of the moral equality of a soldier its force, like the other principles of jus ad bellum and other moral principles in general, is that it is the product of a long history of both moral debate and military practice. In this view, we do not reason our way to judgments about the morality of war privately, but must do so collectively. Put differently, the traditional view does not treat just-war theory as a branch of applied ethics but as a form of role-specific morality. If we want to refute the revisionist conclusions that combatants must make independent judgments of their army's cause, it seems that the most promising route is to query their underlying methodology and teach just-war theory as discontinuous with personal morality and, instead, as dependent on questions in democratic theory. This might lead us to the conclusion that it is, at least sometimes, possible that the Armed Forces are not morally required to make an individual judgment about just cause, but they should be permitted to do so if they cannot accept their state's decision.

CONCLUSION

Generations of students of just-war theory have been taught that states have rights to political sovereignty and to territorial integrity, and that there is a dualism between jus ad bellum and jus in bello, with policy makers responsible for the resort to war, and soldiers and their officers for the conduct of war on the battlefield. In recent decades, a new group of cosmopolitans trained in the techniques of analytic philosophy have challenged these notions, arguing that just wars are indeed defensive ones, but that they defend socially basic human rights, not nation-states, and that ordinary combatants must be held responsible for the cause for which they fight. Underlying both these developments is the view of just wars as a sort of global law enforcement, a view that denies the sovereignty of unjust states, but may also have the effect of eclipsing political activity and moral deliberation on the part of citizens. In surveying this literature, it is suggested that its most important contribution is the emphasis on the seriousness with which taking a life must be regarded, no matter the context in which it is taken. War may be a world apart, but that does not mean that efforts to bring it closer to the ordinary moral world are mere foolishness. However, those efforts must not forget that political pluralism and collective self-determination are also important moral goods and that they are ones for which soldiers continue to be prepared to risk their lives.

The major points that we should take from this survey of cosmopolitan just-war theory are:

- Given the moral risks involved in waging war, institutional reform designed to encourage a more peaceful international system is to be welcomed. In particular, a jus ad bellum branch of the International Criminal Court, which would make advisory rulings on questions of just cause, would bring greater clarity to the murkiness that is the fog of (resort to) war. However, given the importance of democratic participation and the persistence of moral disagreement, the court should only aim to produce advisory judgments that contribute to, but do not determine, the decision to go to war. Likewise, while we should encourage combatants to consider the justice of their army's cause, we should not brand as murderers those who fight for what we later deem to be an unjust cause.
- There is a need for greater incorporation of new cosmopolitan approaches to military ethics in the academies of the Armed Forces, and especially for consideration of the jus ad bellum requirement of just cause within the context of particular wars. This is particularly so because of the question of the concerned method. If we want to reject the revisionist argument that soldiers must make individual judgments of just cause, we will probably have to do so by adopting the view that the role of combatant has its own morality that is discontinuous with interpersonal morality. As a form of role morality, it requires the study not just of ethics, but also of the history and strategy of warfare. Education in military ethics can also usefully be integrated with strategic ends.

- The Armed Forces should at least consider the question of selective conscientious objection. As military discipline is compatible with disobeying illegal jus in bello orders, it might be compatible with disobeying the call to go to war. If, after due consideration, this is deemed potentially disruptive of the effectiveness of the Armed Forces, then the policy on dishonorable discharge should be rethought so that soldiers can resign their commission with honor if their conscience forbids them to participate in a particular war.
- For reasons of space, this question is not considered here, but it is important to note that future research should also consider the question of jus ad vim, or the resort to force short of war. Counterterrorism and covert operations of all kinds are often even more shrouded in secrecy than are wars per se, and they can involve the commission of mortal harm that may turn out to be unjust. This suggests that future research should focus on the morality of obedience to orders to deploy force short of war.

ENDNOTES

1. The classic recent statement of this argument is in Michael Walzer, *Just and Unjust Wars: A Moral Argument with Historical Illustrations*, New York: Basic Books, 2015 (1977), pp. 53-63. Compare to Brian Orend, *The Morality of War*, Peterborough, Ontario, Canada: Broadview Press, 2013, pp. 31-67; and A. J. Coates, *The Ethics of War*, Manchester, United Kingdom: Manchester University Press, 1995, pp. 97-122, 146-166. For a critique of what it takes to be the orthodox view that just wars are wars of national defense, see David Rodin, *War and Self-Defense*, Oxford, UK: Clarendon Press, 2002, pp. 1-13.

2. Walzer, *Just and Unjust Wars*, pp. 121-122.

3. Ibid., p. xxviii.

4. The phrase "socially basic human rights" is from David Luban, "Just War and Human Rights," *Philosophy and Public Affairs*, Vol. 9, No. 2, 1980, pp. 161-181 and p. 175. Compare to Charles Beitz, "Bounded Morality: Justice and the State in World Politics," *International Organization*, Vol. 33, No. 3, 1979, pp. 405-424; Brian Orend, *War and International Justice: A Kantian Perspective*, Waterloo, Ontario, Canada: Wilfrid Laurier University Press, 2000; David Rodin, *War and Self-Defense*; and Jeff McMahan, *Killing in War*, Oxford, UK: Clarendon Press, 2009.

5. See McMahan, *Killing in War*, and Jeff McMahan, "The Morality of War and the Law of War," in David Rodin and Henry Shue, eds., *Just and Unjust Warriors: The Moral and Legal Status of Soldiers*, Oxford, UK: Oxford University Press, 2008, pp. 19-43; Rodin, *War and Self-Defense*, and David Rodin, "The Moral Inequality of Soldiers: Why jus in bello Asymmetry is Half Right," in Rodin and Shue, eds., *Just and Unjust Warriors*, pp. 44-68. Compare to Cheyney Ryan, "Moral Equality, Victimhood, and the Sovereignty Symmetry Problem," in Rodin and Shue, eds., *Just and Unjust Warriors*, pp. 131-152; Judith Lichtenberg, "How to Judge Soldiers Whose Cause is Unjust," in Rodin and Shue, eds., *Just and Unjust Warriors*, pp. 112-131; Cécile Fabre, "Cosmopolitanism and Wars of Self-Defense," in Cécile Fabre and Seth Lazar, eds., *The Morality of Defensive War*, Oxford, UK: Oxford University Press, 2014, pp. 90-114; and Lionel McPherson, "Innocence and

Responsibility in War," *Canadian Journal of Philosophy*, Vol. 34, No. 4, 2004, pp. 485-506.

6. Walzer, *Just and Unjust Wars*, pp. 38-39.

7. Ibid., pp. 34-37.

8. Lichtenberg, "How to Judge Soldiers," p. 112.

9. Rodin, *War and Self-Defense*, pp. 70-79; McMahan, *Killing in War*, pp. 32-37.

10. Rodin, *War and Self-Defense*, pp. 26-34, 90-99; McMahan, *Killing in War*, pp. 104-154. Compare to Lichtenberg, "How to Judge Soldiers," pp. 114-125; Ryan, "Moral Equality," pp. 139-141. On the legal distinction between excuse and justification, see George Fletcher, *Rethinking Criminal Law*, Boston, MA: Little Brown, 1978, ch. 10. For critiques of this argument, see Michael Walzer, "The Political Theory License," *Annual Review of Political Science*, 2013, pp. 1-9; and *Just and Unjust Wars*, pp. 335-346.

11. See Rodin, "The Moral Inequality of Soldiers," pp. 44-45, for the connection between these claims.

12. McMahan, *Killing in War*, pp. 95-103. For earlier arguments about selective conscientious objection, see Paul Ramsey, *The Just War: Force and Political Responsibility*, New York: Charles Scribner, 1968, pp. 91-137; and Michael Walzer, *Obligations: Essays on Disobedience, War, and Citizenship*, Cambridge, MA: Harvard University Press, 1970, pp. 120-145.

13. On this, see Jeff McMahan, "The Prevention of Unjust Wars," in Yitzhak Benbaji and Naomi Sussmann, eds., *Reading Walzer*, New York: Routledge, 2013, pp. 233-255. For critique, see Yitzhak Benbaji, "Against a Cosmopolitan Institutionalization of Just War," in Benbaji and Sussmann, eds., *Reading Walzer*, pp. 256-276.

14. Beitz, "Bounded Morality"; Luban, "Just War and Human Rights"; Richard Wasserstrom, "Review of Michael Walzer's Just and Unjust Wars," *Harvard Law Review,* Vol. 92, No. 2, 1978, pp. 536-545; and Gerald Doppelt, "Walzer's Theory of Morality in

International Relations," *Philosophy and Public Affairs*, Vol. 8, No. 1, 1978, pp. 3-26.

15. See Orend, *The Morality of War*, pp. 160-219; Orend, *Michael Walzer on War and Justice*, Cardiff, UK: University of Wales Press, 2000, pp. 135-152; Eric Patterson, *Ending Wars Well: Order, Justice, and Conciliation in Contemporary Post-Conflict*, New Haven, CT: Yale University Press, 2012; Eric Patterson, ed., *Ethics Beyond War's End*, Washington, DC: Georgetown University Press, 2012; and Mark Evans, "Moral Responsibilities and the Conflicting Demands of Jus Post Bellum," *Ethics and International Affairs*, Vol. 23, No. 2, 2009, pp. 147-164.

16. The literature on jus ad bellum is vast. The following accounts include most, but not all, of the principles stated here: Orend, *The Morality of War*, chs. 2-3; Walzer, *Just and Unjust Wars*, chs. 2, 4-7; Coates, *The Ethics of War*, chs. 4-8; Nigel Dower, *The Ethics of War and Peace: Cosmopolitan and Other Perspectives*, London, UK: Polity, 2009, pp. 81-94; David Kinsella and Craig Carr, eds., *The Morality of War: A Reader*, Boulder, CO: Lynne Rienner, 2007, chs. 5-6. For an accessible brief introduction, see the *Stanford Encyclopedia of Philosophy's* entry on War in sec. 2.1, available from *https://plato.stanford.edu/entries/war/#HistVsContJustWarTheo*, accessed October 18, 2016. Compare to James Turner Johnson, *Just War Tradition and the Restraint of War: A Moral and Historical Inquiry*, Princeton, NJ: Princeton University Press, 2014 (1981); William O'Brien, *The Conduct of Just and Limited War*, New York: Praeger, 1981; and Ramsey, *The Just War*.

17. On jus in bello, see Orend, *The Morality of War*, ch. 4; Walzer, *Just and Unjust Wars*, chs. 3, 8-13; Coates, *The Ethics of War*, chs. 9-10; Dower, *Ethics of War and Peace*, pp. 94-97. Compare to the *Stanford Encyclopedia of Philosophy's* entry on war, sec. 2.2.

18. As we shall see, one of the disagreements among the new revisionist just-war theorists concerns whether rejecting the moral equality of soldiers means calling into question the principle of non-combatant immunity. McMahan suggests that, in principle, it does. Rodin rejects this claim in "The Moral Inequality of Soldiers," pp. 54-64. Compare to C. A. J. Coady, "The Status of Combatants," in Rodin and Shue, eds., *Just and Unjust Warriors*, pp. 153-175.

19. For a brief history of just-war theory, see Orend, *The Morality of War*, ch. 1. A similar distinction also appears in the more recent Christian just-war theory of Elizabeth Anscombe, "Just War: The Case of World War II," in Robert Goodin, Philip Pettit, and Thomas Pogge, eds., *Contemporary Political Philosophy: An Anthology*, Oxford, UK: Blackwell, 2006, pp. 623-635. However, compare to Gregory Reichberg, "Just War and Regular War: Competing Paradigms," in Rodin and Shue, eds., *Just and Unjust Warriors*, pp. 193-213. Reichberg rejects the claim that traditional just-war theory did not require ordinary combatants to assess the justice of their side's cause.

20. Rodin, "The Moral Inequality of Soldiers," p. 44. Compare to Rodin, "The Ethics of Asymmetric War," in Richard Sorabji and David Rodin, eds., *The Ethics of War: Shared Problems in Different Traditions*, London, UK: Ashgate, 2006, pp. 153-168.

21. Walzer, *Just and Unjust Wars*, p. 34.

22. Ibid., p. 36. On the crime of war, see pp. 21-33.

23. Ibid., p. 127.

24. Ibid.

25. Ibid., pp. 37-41.

26. Ibid., pp. 228-232, 242-249.

27. Ibid., p. 231.

28. Rodin, "The Moral Inequality of Soldiers," pp. 54-56. Rodin rejects "permissive asymmetry," pp. 47-51.

29. Walzer, *Just and Unjust Wars*, pp. 250-267.

30. Ibid., p. 252.

31. I have addressed this question previously in J. Toby Reiner, "'Supreme Emergencies,' ontological holism, and rights to communal membership," *Critical Review of International Social and Political Philosophy*, Vol. 20, Iss. 4, 2017, pub. online March 10, 2015, available from *https://www.tandfonline.com/doi/abs/10.1080/13698230.2015.1004837*. Important critiques of Walzer's position

include Alex Bellamy, "Supreme Emergencies and the Protection of Non-Combatants in War," *International Affairs*, Vol. 80, No. 5, 2004, pp. 829-850; C. A. J. Coady, "Terrorism, Morality, and Supreme Emergency," *Ethics*, Vol. 114, No. 4, 2004, pp. 772-789; Martin Cook, "Michael Walzer's Concept of 'Supreme Emergency'," *Journal of Military Ethics*, Vol. 6, No. 2, 2007, pp. 138-151; Henry Shue, "Liberalism: The Impossibility of Justifying Weapons of Mass Destruction," in Sohail H. Hashmi and Steven P. Lee, eds., *Ethics and Weapons of Mass Destruction: Religious and Secular Perspectives*, Cambridge, UK: Cambridge University Press, 2004, pp. 139-162; and Christopher Toner, "Just War and the Supreme Emergency Exemption," *The Philosophical Quarterly*, Vol. 55, 2005, pp. 545-561.

32. Again, revisionists sometimes go further in this regard. Rodin rejects the claim that wars of national defense are justified at all, and assimilates war to a law-enforcement model. See Rodin, *War and Self-Defense*, chs. 7-8.

33. For these criticisms, see the references in this volume's endnote 14. For a more recent version of the debate, see Ruth Gavison, "Taking states seriously," Charles Beitz, "The Moral Standing of States revisited," and Michael Doyle, "A few words on Mill, Walzer, and nonintervention," in Benbaji and Sussmann, eds., *Reading Walzer*, pp. 40-60, 61-82, 83-103, respectively.

34. Michael Walzer, "The Moral Standing of States: A Response to Four Critics," *Philosophy and Public Affairs*, Vol. 9, No. 3, 1980, pp. 209-229, reprinted in Michael Walzer, *Thinking Politically: Essays in Political Theory*, New Haven, CT: Yale University Press, 2007, p. 225.

35. Walzer, "The Moral Standing of States," pp. 233-234. Compare to *Just and Unjust Wars*, p. 61.

36. Walzer, *Just and Unjust Wars*, pp. 58-63. For Beitz's account of this as the heart of their disagreement, see "The Moral Standing of States Revisited."

37. Walzer, "The Moral Standing of States," p. 234.

38. Beitz, "The Moral Standing of States Revisited," p. 68. For the rejoinders to Walzer, see Charles Beitz, "Nonintervention and

Communal Integrity," David Luban, "The Romance of the Nation State," and Gerald Doppelt, "Statism without Foundations," *Philosophy and Public Affairs*, Vol. 9, No. 4, 1980, pp. 385-391, 392-397, 398-403, respectively.

39. Luban, "Just War," p. 175. For a definition and analysis of the notion of basic rights, see Henry Shue, *Basic Rights: Subsistence, Affluence, and U.S. Foreign Policy*, Princeton, NJ: Princeton University Press, 1980.

40. Luban, "The Romance of the Nation State," p. 392.

41. Ibid., p. 393.

42. Walzer, "The Moral Standing of States," p. 227.

43. For more information on this issue, see Ibid., pp. 226-228; and Luban, "Just War," pp. 170-171.

44. These reflections on jus post bellum are necessarily brief. I plan to expand this analysis in a future monograph.

45. Patterson, ed., *Ethics Beyond War's End*, pp. 7-8.

46. Ibid., p. 11.

47. Walzer, *Just and Unjust Wars*, p. 122.

48. Ibid.

49. Ibid., p. 123.

50. For discussion of this point, see Michael Walzer, "The Argument about Humanitarian Intervention," in Walzer, *Thinking Politically*, pp. 246-247.

51. By this, I do not just mean that his views have become dominant, but that his project is to systematize the prevailing moral conceptions that currently guide practice, not to formulate the ideal ones that should do so. That is why he appeals to the "moral reality" of war. On this, see Walzer, *Just and Unjust Wars*, pp. 13-16. For an argument that this is Walzer's general method of theorizing, see J. Toby Reiner, "Social Meanings and the Cultural

Theory of Goods in Michael Walzer's Ethical Anthropology," *Polity*, Vol. 48, No. 3, July 2016, pp. 359-386.

52. On this point, see Patterson, ed., *Ethics Beyond War's End*, pp. 7-8.

53. For an account of the Nuremberg Trials as central to the development of a theory of jus post bellum, see Kinsella and Carr, eds., *The Morality of War*, pp. 343-358.

54. Walzer, *Just and Unjust Wars*, pp. 287-303. See also pp. 304-327.

55. The editor makes this suggestion in Patterson, ed., *Ethics Beyond War's End*, p. 7.

56. Ibid., pp. 5-9.

57. Walzer, "The Argument about Humanitarian Intervention," pp. 247-248. Compare to Michael Walzer and Nicolaus Mills, eds., *Getting Out: Historical Perspectives on Leaving Iraq*, Philadelphia, PA: University of Pennsylvania Press, 2009.

58. Michael Walzer, "The Aftermath of War: Reflections on *Jus Post Bellum*," in Patterson, ed., *Ethics Beyond War's End*, p. 45.

59. Brian Orend, "Justice After War: Toward a New Geneva Convention," in Patterson, ed., *Ethics Beyond War's End*, pp. 175-195 and pp. 183-184. Compare to Orend, *The Morality of War*, pp. 160-189, and "Justice After War," *Ethics and International Affairs*, Vol. 16, No. 1, 2002, pp. 43-56.

60. See Patterson, ed., *Ethics Beyond War's End*, pp. ix-x, 1-4, 9-15. Compare to Eric Patterson, "*Jus Post Bellum* and International Conflict: Order, Justice, and Reconciliation," in Michael Brough, John Lango, and Harry van der Linden, eds., *Rethinking the Just War Tradition*, Albany, NY: State University of New York Press, 2007, pp. 35-52.

61. Orend, "Justice After War: Toward a New Geneva Convention," pp. 179-181.

62. Ibid., pp. 182-183.

63. Ibid., p. 187.

64. It maintains the view that just wars are limited in their means.

65. Mark Evans, "'Just Peace': An Elusive Ideal," in Patterson, ed., *Ethics Beyond War's End*, p. 206. Compare to Mark Evans, "Moral Responsibilities and the Conflicting Demands of *Jus Post Bellum*," *Ethics and International Affairs*, Vol. 23, No. 2, 2009, p. 147-164.

66. Evans, "Just Peace," p. 210.

67. On this, see George Lucas, "*Jus Ante* and *Post Bellum:* Completing the Circle, Breaking the Cycle," in Patterson, ed., *Ethics Beyond War's End*, pp. 47-164.

68. For examples, see James Turner Johnson, "Moral Responsibility After Conflict: The Idea of *Jus Post Bellum* for the Twenty-First Century," in Patterson, ed., *Ethics Beyond War's End*, pp. 31-32. Compare to Benbaji, "Against a Cosmopolitan Institutionalization of Just War," pp. 256-276. On the conception of war as law enforcement or policing, see Caroline Holmqvist, *Policing Wars: On Military Intervention in the Twenty-First Century*, London, UK: Palgrave Macmillan, 2014.

69. For more information on this issue, see Orend, *The Morality of War*, chs. 6-7.

70. Walzer, *Just and Unjust Wars*, pp. 152-159. Compare to Michael Walzer, *Arguing Against War*, New Haven, CT: Yale University Press, 2004, pp. 3-32.

71. Walzer, *Just and Unjust Wars*, pp. 152-154.

72. Rodin, *War and Self-Defense*, pp. 1-2; McMahan, *Killing in War*, pp. vii-viii.

73. McMahan, *Killing in War*, p. 14.

74. Rodin, *War and Self-Defense*, p. 163.

75. McMahan, *Killing in War*, pp. 32-37; Rodin, *War and Self-Defense*, p. 164.

76. McMahan, *Killing in War*, pp. 9-15, compare to pp. 162-174; Rodin, *War and Self-Defense*, pp. 77-83; Rodin, "The Moral Inequality of Soldiers," pp. 45-47; compare to Lichtenberg, "How to Judge Soldiers," pp. 114-148; Coady, "The Status of Combatants," pp. 155-156; Frederik Kaufman, "Just War Theory and Killing the Innocent," *Rethinking the Just War Tradition*, pp. 99-100. For a critique, see Christopher Kutz, "Fearful Symmetry," in Rodin and Shue, eds., *Just and Unjust Warriors*, pp. 81-85. For Walzer's usage of innocence, see *Just and Unjust Wars*, pp. 144-147.

77. For reasons of space, my coverage is limited. For a fuller account, see McMahan, *Killing in War*, pp. 38-103, which is devoted to the consideration of the arguments for the moral equality of combatants and McMahan's objections to them, such as lack of knowledge, duties to defer to their government or sustain shared institutions, and the fact that we do not require soldiers to take up arms for a just cause.

78. Rodin, *War and Self-Defense*, pp. 169-170. McMahan makes a similar argument in *Killing in War*, pp. 143-145. Compare to Ryan, "Moral Equality," pp. 146-147.

79. On the distinction between excuse and justification, see Rodin, *War and Self-Defense*, pp. 26-34. Compare to McMahan's distinction between excuse and permission in *Killing in War*, pp. 110-115.

80. McMahan, *Killing in War*, pp. 112-113, 116-118.

81. For more on this, see McMahan, *Killing in War*, pp. 131-137. Compare to Lichtenberg, "How to Judge Soldiers," pp. 118-122; Ryan, "Moral Equality," pp. 139-141; and Rodin, *War and Self-Defense*, pp. 170-173.

82. Walzer, *Just and Unjust Wars*, p. 127. See this volume's endnote 25.

83. McMahan, *Killing in War*, pp. 119-122.

84. Ibid., p. 137.

85. Ibid., pp. 137-154.

86. Ibid., p. 141.

87. Ibid., p. 142.

88. Ibid., pp. 144-145.

89. Ibid., p. 145.

90. Ibid., p. 152.

91. Rodin, *War and Self-Defense*, p. 166.

92. Ibid., pp. 166-168.

93. This is the major theme of Ryan, "Moral Equality." See especially pp. 144-146. For a different view, see Dan Zupan, "A Presumption of the Moral Equality of Combatants: A Citizen-Soldier's Perspective," in Rodin and Shue, eds., *Just and Unjust Warriors*, pp. 214-225.

94. McMahan, *Killing in War*, pp. 11-12.

95. Ibid., pp. 203-218.

96. Ibid., pp. 214-215, 221-222.

97. Ibid., p. 222.

98. Ibid.

99. Ibid., p. 231.

100. Ibid., p. 234. Compare to McMahan, "The Morality of War and the Law of War," and McMahan, "The Prevention of Unjust Wars."

101. Rodin, "The Moral Inequality of Soldiers," p. 56.

102. Rodin suggests that just wars should be viewed as a form of global law enforcement in *War and Self-Defense*, pp. 173-179.

103. McMahan, *Killing in War*, p. 97.

104. Ibid., p. 136.

105. Michael Walzer, "Response," in Benbaji and Sussmann, eds., *Reading Walzer*, pp. 328-332.

106. Robert Nozick, *Anarchy, State, and Utopia*, New York: Basic Books, 1974, p. 100. Walzer objects to this argument in *Just and Unjust Wars*, p. 40, arguing that moral sensitivity should lead us to recognize that "authority structures and socialization processes" are sufficiently strong as to negate the requirement of individualized judgements of the justice of an army's cause.

107. Orend, *Michael Walzer on War and Justice*, p. 114.

108. Nozick, *Anarchy, State, and Utopia*, p. x.

109. Walzer, *Just and Unjust Wars*, pp. 335-346. Compare to Walzer, "The Political Theory License."

110. Walzer, *Just and Unjust Wars*, pp. 127-128.

111. Ibid., p. 339.

112. Ibid., p. 340.

113. Ibid., p. 343.

114. Ibid., p. 337.

115. Ibid., pp. 335-336.

116. Ibid., pp. 61-63.

117. McMahan, *Killing in War*, p. vii. I believe that the same is true of Rodin, who defines the central tenet of revisionist just-war theory as being, "the claim that human rights do not stop at the edge of the battlefield, but rather apply to all persons in all circumstances." Quote from a closed Facebook group: Just War Theory Group, October 5, 2016.

118. On this point, I am grateful for private correspondence with Michael Walzer.

119. On this, see McMahan, "The Morality of War and the Law of War." For critique, see Henry Shue, "Do We Need a 'Morality of War'?" in Rodin and Shue, eds., *Just and Unjust Warriors*, pp. 87-111.

120. McMahan, "The Prevention of Unjust Wars," quote at p. 242. Compare to Benbaji, "Against a Cosmopolitan Institutionalization of Just War," and Walzer, "Response."

121. Rodin, *War and Self-Defense*, pp. 179-180.

122. Ibid., pp. 179-188.

123. McMahan, "The Prevention of Unjust Wars," pp. 252-253.

124. Ibid., p. 248.

125. Walzer, "Response," p. 330.

126. McMahan, "The Prevention of Unjust Wars," pp. 248-249.

127. On this, see Benbaji, "Against a Cosmopolitan Institutionalization of Just War," pp. 264-274.

128. Ibid., pp. 269-271.

129. Ibid., p. 272.

130. Ibid., pp. 272-273.

131. Walzer, "Response," pp. 331-332.

132. Most notably, Benbaji, "Against a Cosmopolitan Institutionalization of Just War." Compare to Yitzhak Benbaji, "The Moral Power of Soldiers to Undertake the Duty of Obedience," *Ethics*, Vol. 122, No. 1, 2011, pp. 41-73; Dan Zupan, "A Presumption of the Moral Equality of Combatants: A Citizen-Soldier's Perspective," in Rodin and Shue, eds., *Just and Unjust Warriors*, pp. 214-225; Michael Brough, "Dehumanization of the Enemy and the Moral Equality of Soldiers," *Rethinking the Just War Tradition*, pp. 149-167.

133. McMahan, *Killing in War*, p. 95.

134. Ibid., pp. 66-84. Compare to Rodin, *War and Self-Defense*, pp. 165-173.

135. Walzer, *Just and Unjust Wars*, pp. 13-16.

136. McMahan, *Killing in War*, p. 98.

137. See for example Walzer's discussion of the My Lai massacre in *Just and Unjust Wars*, pp. 309-316.

138. McMahan, *Killing in War*, p. 98.

139. Michael Walzer, *Obligations: Essays on Disobedience, War, and Citizenship*, Cambridge, MA: Harvard University Press, 1970, ch. 6. Walzer points this out in "Response," p. 331.

140. Rodin, *War and Self-Defense*, pp. 83-88; McMahan, *Killing in War*, especially pp. 60-62, 162-167.

141. See, for example, Walzer, *Just and Unjust Wars*, p. 298. Compare to Reiner, "Social Meanings."

U.S. ARMY WAR COLLEGE

Major General John S. Kem
Commandant

*****

STRATEGIC STUDIES INSTITUTE
AND
U.S. ARMY WAR COLLEGE PRESS

Director
Professor Douglas C. Lovelace, Jr.

Director of Research
Dr. Steven K. Metz

Author
Dr. J. Toby Reiner

Editor for Production
Dr. James G. Pierce

Publications Assistant
Ms. Denise J. Kersting

*****

Composition
Mrs. Jennifer E. Nevil

Made in the USA
Middletown, DE
02 November 2022

13948279R00050